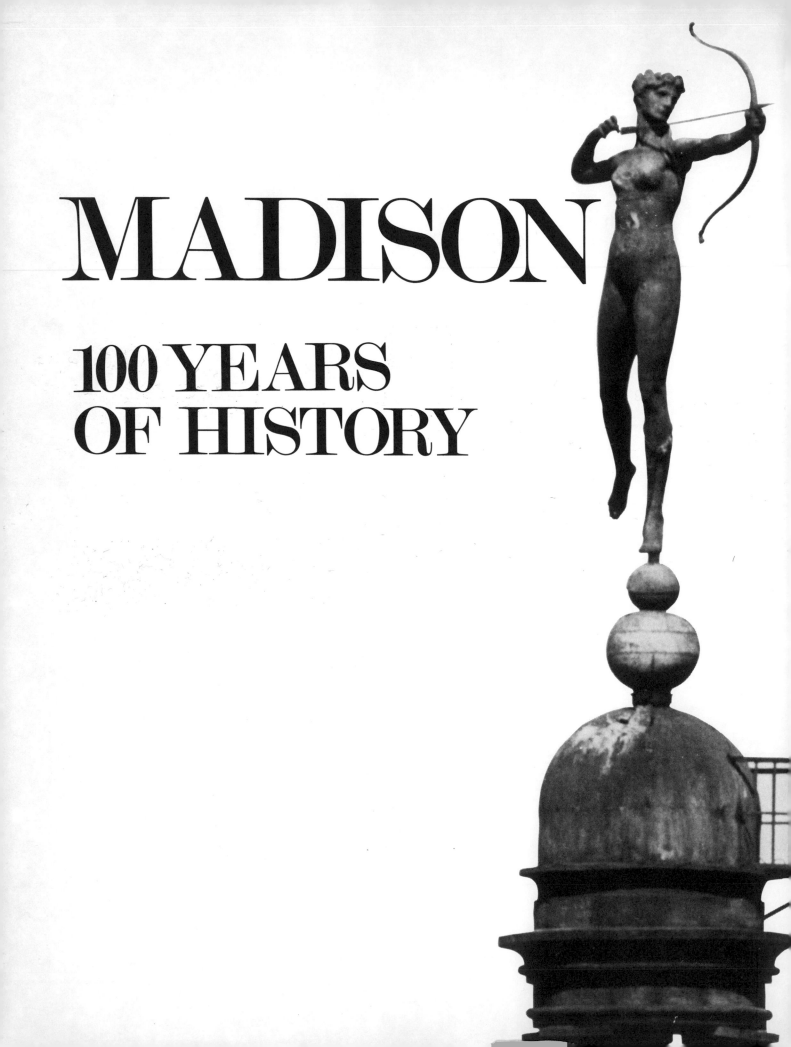

MADISON

100 YEARS
OF HISTORY

SQUARE GARDEN

by Joseph Durso

SIMON AND SCHUSTER

NEW YORK

PHOTO CREDITS:

CULVER PICTURES: 16, 19, 20, 21, 32, 36, 37, 40, 52, 68.

GEORGE KALINSKY, MADISON SQUARE GARDEN: 178 (top), 179, 180 (top), 181, 185, 211, 214 (left), 218, 223, 224, 225, 226, 229, 230–31, 239, 240, 241, 242, 244, 245, 249, 250, 251, 252, 253, 254, 255.

MADISON SQUARE GARDEN: 48, 81, 94, 99, 130, 131, 141, 142, 143, 146, 147, 148, 158, 167, 171 (top left), 178 (bottom), 182, 194, 198, 210, 212, 213, 214 (top right and bottom right), 235, 237, 243, 247, 248.

NEW YORK LIFE INSURANCE COMPANY ARCHIVES: 12, 14, 22, 28, 29, 45, 50, 55, 70, 74, 75, 76, 86, 90, 92, 100, 101, 136.

UNITED PRESS INTERNATIONAL: 17, 18, 24, 26, 27, 30, 33, 35, 39, 42, 46, 58, 59, 63, 65, 66, 69, 73, 78, 80, 83, 89, 91, 102, 103, 105, 106, 107, 110, 111, 112, 113, 116, 119, 121, 125, 127, 132, 133, 135, 139, 151, 153, 154, 159, 162, 165, 166, 168, 169, 171 (bottom right), 172, 174, 176, 177, 180 (bottom), 190, 191, 195, 196, 197, 199, 200, 206.

COLOR PHOTO SECTION BY GEORGE KALINSKY

Published by Simon and Schuster
A Division of Gulf & Western Corporation
Simon & Schuster Building
Rockefeller Center
1230 Avenue of the Americas
New York, New York 10020

Designed by Stanley S. Drate
Photo editor: Vincent Virga
Manufactured in the United States of America
Printed by The Murray Printing Company
Bound by The Book Press, Inc.
1 2 3 4 5 6 7 8 9 10

Library of Congress Cataloging in Publication Data

Durso, Joseph.
   Madison Square Garden, 100 years of history.

   1. New York (City). Madison Square Garden—History.
I. Title.
GV416.N485D87   790.2'09747'1   79-14687

ISBN 0-671-24425-6

BOOKS BY JOSEPH DURSO

Casey: The Life and Legend of Charles Dillon Stengel
The Days of Mr. McGraw
Amazing: The Miracle of the Mets
The All-American Dollar
Yankee Stadium: Fifty Years of Drama
Screwball (with Tug McGraw)
The Sports Factory
My Luke and I (with Mrs. Lou Gehrig)
Whitey and Mickey (with Whitey Ford and Mickey Mantle)

Contents

Acknowledgments

To those of us who grew up hearing adventures of "the good old days," few places in America seemed to hold more adventures than Madison Square Garden in any of its four buildings in three locations in New York. And no one was more spellbinding in describing the adventures than my father, who enlivened the cold Adirondack nights with personal recollections of giants like Jack Dempsey and Tex Rickard.

So, in tracing the history of that "state of mind" called the Garden, my acknowledgments start with him. Without his zest for life and its folk heroes and foibles, there is no telling where the path would have led. But it led here and, with the help and guidance of many other persons, I have tried to recapture the history of that crowded stage and the people who crossed it.

Starting at the top, my thanks go to the current keepers of the keys: Sonny Werblin, the boss of bosses, who shared his thoughts and his productions as he did in football, horse racing, and his numerous other interests; and Michael Burke, whom I first encountered when he was overseeing the New York Yankees for the Columbia Broadcasting System and whose career is a series of adventures in itself. They opened the doors to the world within, no strings attached.

My thanks also to their colleagues, starting with Joel Nixon, "the man in the red baseball cap" at ringside before he became senior vice-president backstage, where he steered me for months through the corridors and even the closets and especially the casts. And to Harry Markson, who did more and remembered more than almost anybody else and who told it in pungent language, from Joe Louis to Muhammad Ali.

9

They were abetted by John Condon, John Goldner, Dick Donopria, Ned Irish, and John and Janet Halligan, without whom the Garden—as well as this history of it—would be poorer. And a special salute to George Kalinsky, the Garden's talented photographer, whose pictures fill this book with the sights and spectacles of the past.

When we had to dig deeper for the sights of the past, they were provided by Nat Andriani and Tommy Gilbert of United Press International's Compix library. The New York Historical Society also filled in some gaps, as did Fred Phelps, a friend with an eye on history, and a pair of past stage performers with long memories: Teddy Hayes, who saw it happen from Jack Dempsey's corner, and James R. Fair, who roared through the Nineteen Twenties with Harry Greb and is now the resident laureate back home in New Martinsville, West Virginia.

Finally, there are the archaeologists of New York Life, which held the mortgage and even the destiny of Madison Square Garden earlier in this century. Jacob Underhill, a reformed political reporter who rose to vice-chairman of New York Life, shared with me the treasures in the company's records on lower Madison Avenue, where the first and second Gardens were situated and where New York Life now has its headquarters. And Pamela Dunn Lehrer, the archivist for the company, brought alive the history of New York in the Victorian era, and did it with insight and skill.

Along with Jonathan Segal, senior editor of Simon and Schuster, who pursues research many evenings from a courtside seat, they form my Madison Square Garden team, and my muse.

—Joseph Durso

. . . a hippodrome, theatre, ballroom,
restaurant, concert hall and summer
garden . . . a sort of pleasure exchange
or central palace of pleasure.
                              Harper's Weekly

1 BARNUM'S MONSTER CLASSICAL AND GEOLOGICAL HIPPODROME

In an age of fantasy, no one captures the public fancy like P. T. Barnum, and no place captures it like his Grand Roman Hippodrome in New York, the forerunner of the many stages of Madison Square Garden.

In 1879 Rutherford B. Hayes was president, Victoria was queen, John L. Sullivan was growing into "the Boston Strong Boy" who could lick any man in the house, Alexander Graham Bell's telephone and the National League of Professional Baseball Clubs were three years old, and Billy the Kid was twenty and not long for this world.

It was only fourteen summers after Appomattox, and America was caught somewhere between the Frontier and the Machine Age, along with the great waves of immigration from Europe that would transform the former into the latter. It was a time when the animals and even the people who had settled the country were being crowded by the inventions that would soon mechanize the country. A time when the Common Man still outnumbered the uncommon man. When the population was soaring from 50 million souls to 75 million in one generation, when everybody was starting to cling to life's lost fantasies.

Only a decade earlier, Gen. Philip H. Sheridan had calculated that 100 million American bison roamed the plains of Kansas and the Indian Territory; only a decade later, an official census of the one-ton buffalo placed the herd somehow at precisely 1,091.

This was also the decade of Custer's Last Stand, when the Indian took no nonsense; but a decade later, at a place called Wounded Knee, the Indian took no comfort. They described it as "the last armed conflict" between the white man and the red man, and the Census Bureau announced that there was no longer a land frontier.

Whatever they termed it, things were changing. Soon after Bell's telephone came Mergenthaler's Linotype and Parsons's steam turbine. Then Edison began lighting the streets, Daimler produced his high-speed internal-combustion engine, Eastman his hand camera, and Otis his electric elevator. By then, country folks were heading for the cities, and "Baltimore, by 1890," Henry L. Mencken observed a little unkindly, "was fast degenerating, and so was civilization."

It was a time when the imagination of the crowd was likely to be captured by impresarios who could keep alive the romance of "the good old days." For example, Phineas Taylor Barnum, the promoter of the folk heroes Tom Thumb and Jenny Lind,

Barnum pitches his tent on the site of the New York & New Haven Railroad depot on the west side of Fourth Avenue, where the city's life flows past Madison Square.

and a man of timeless fantasy who soon joined forces with his archrival, James Anthony Bailey, to form the great traveling circus that for generations trouped across the changing nation.

So by 1879, while the country was outgrowing its past and its wilderness, Barnum was busy providing not only the liveliest stage in town but also the acts to keep it lively. The town was New York, and the stage took shape three blocks north of the Manhattan intersection where Twenty-third Street crossed both Fifth Avenue and Broadway. They called it Madison Square, for the fourth president of the United States, James Madison.

But Barnum's chief interest centered on the northeast corner of the square, precisely on the old railroad shed where the New

York & Harlem Railroad used to stable its horses—which were required by city ordinance to draw the railroad cars north to Thirty-second Street before surrendering them to mechanical power.

And it was there, just off the little park of Madison Square, that Barnum led his elephants and quartered them for the fantasies they helped keep alive against the tide of "modern times." He was not the sort who would skimp on either brain power or word power, and he promptly acclaimed his own dazzling enterprise "the Monster Classical and Geological Hippodrome."

It became, the *New York Herald Tribune* suggested during the century that followed, "not a building, but a state of mind."

Madison Square, they called it. Four and a half acres of Manhattan Island off Fifth Avenue, starting at Twenty-third Street and extending north three blocks. It was set aside as a park in 1836 by the City Council of New York, which also ponied up $2,000 for seeding the soil, and before long the local guidebooks were calling it "the central point of life and splendor in uptown New York." That's right: *uptown* New York.

Part of its splendor came from the fashionable young sports who gathered there in the afternoon to pursue the leisure hours, which were pursued chiefly by fashionable young sports because most other people were trapped inside the factories and sweatshops created by the Industrial Revolution. They were not your run-of-the-mill street-corner gang; nothing like that. They were well heeled and well motivated, and they even endowed themselves with a name that proved to be somewhat prophetic—the Knickerbocker Base Ball and Social Club.

Their game, baseball (usually written as two words), was related to any number of other pastimes that involved hitting a round ball with a wooden stick. In other places, on other continents, inside other parks, it could be identified with cricket, rounders, one o'cat, and even town ball, a kind of mass mayhem that pitted almost everybody in one town against everybody in a neighboring town—with a passion.

To keep the passion more or less in bounds, a new set of rules was drawn up by one of the young sports of the club, Alexander Joy Cartwright. It seemed a little inane to Cartwright that the sport took as many forms as, say, poker in later years —with the ball games, in some cases, going on until somebody

The park at Madison Square has already become the center of Manhattan's social and sporting life, the place where Alexander Joy Cartwright laid out the first baseball diamond for the Knickerbocker Club.

It is named for the fourth President of the United States, James Madison, and already it's known as "the central point of life and splendor in uptown New York."

scored twenty-one runs. So he worked out his new rules, and not bad, at that: placing the bases ninety feet apart in the general design of a diamond, three "outs" to each side in an "inning," and nine innings to a ball game.

Having established the geometry, the Knickerbocker Base Ball and Social Club promptly blew the opportunity. In the first match on record, the young dudes of Madison Square took their game across the Hudson River to another historic lot in Hoboken, New Jersey. And there, on the grandly named Elysian Fields, with Cartwright serving as the umpire, they went four calamitous innings against a rival club, the New York Nine. Final score: 23–1.

Now, in the Victorian Era, in the years after the Civil War, Rutherford B. Hayes occupies the White House . . .

But the real splendor of Madison Square grew along the fringes of the park, where town houses began to rise across the avenue from Cartwright's "diamond." One of the most lavish was the red brick and white marble mansion of Leonard Jerome, part owner of the *New York Times* and later the grandfather of Winston Churchill. And, by the start of the Civil War, these houses were flanked by luxury hotels—the St. James, the Hoffman House, the Albemarle, and the seven-story Fifth Avenue Hotel.

One exception to the palatial quality of the neighborhood, though, stood rather starkly on the northeast edge of the square, between Twenty-sixth and Twenty-seventh streets in the block between Fourth and Madison avenues. It was the freight shed and stable of the New York & Harlem Railroad, along with a passenger depot that did nothing to add much grace to the scene.

But that problem was solved in 1871, when "Commodore" Cornelius Vanderbilt shifted the railroad operations sixteen blocks north to Grand Central Terminal, thereby opening the square to the showmanship of P. T. Barnum. Two years later Barnum leased the abandoned rail station, spent $35,000 to rebuild the depot, circled it with a 28-foot brick wall, and created an open yard that measured 425 feet by 200 feet. Then came the *pièce de résistance*—an elliptical arena 270 feet long with rows of wooden seats and the most imaginative "stage" in town.

Then, on April 27, 1874, he rang up the curtain on the Great Roman Hippodrome, or, if that sounded a bit too simple for such a whirlwind scheme, Barnum's Monster Classical and Geological Hippodrome.

To behold the wonders inside—and 15,000 people at a time converged on the square to do just that—all you had to do was pay Barnum the significant sum of one American dollar. In return, the great man rewarded the senses with more action than the city or the square had beheld since the Dutch haggled with the Indians a couple of centuries earlier. Chariots with lady drivers raced over the turf. Japanese acrobats tumbled through the air. Cowboys chased Indians, and Indians chased cowboys. Freaks devoured fire or exhibited their tattooed bodies. Actors portrayed the many lives and many wives of Bluebeard the ogre. The flags of the Congress of Nations flapped in the breeze. Arabian horses pranced and elephants waltzed to the music.

For three months Barnum kept the magic flowing before taking his show on the road. When he returned to New York, he was dismayed to find winter gripping the square, but he executed a shrewd about-face and headed south with his freaks and animals while the lease was being auctioned off. The winner: Patrick Sarsfield Gilmore, the bandmaster, who did nothing to diminish the splendor, either.

Gilmore, it might be said, even injected a little "tone" to the setting: fountains, statues, potted azaleas, gravel walks. And naturally, in the absence now of monsters, classical or geological, he retitled the edifice with no more modesty than Barnum, calling it simply and subjectively Gilmore's Garden.

It was a far cry from Cartwright's ninety-foot bases and Barnum's elephants, but Gilmore had the ball now and he ran with it. He staged revival meetings led by the evangelists Dwight L. Moody and Ira D. Sankey. He produced temperance meetings and, if they threatened to be too dull, followed them with policemen's balls. Then a beauty contest, flower exhibits, return appearances by Barnum's traveling circus and, in 1877, the first Westminster Kennel Show—the "first annual New York bench show" for dogs, including one named Sprite, who was entered in the "trick dog class" without pedigree papers but with a price tag of $200.

Gilmore's Garden was still chiefly an outdoor arena, and the arrival of winter sent the same chill through the air that Barnum had felt—and fled. But Gilmore held his ground and turned to a sure crowd-pleaser: boxing. Never mind that New York State law threatened arrest for anyone who took part in "a contention with fists." He simply removed the contention and left the fists.

They were called "exhibitions" or, better yet, "illustrated lectures," with the "professors" appearing in tights and wearing gloves that the *New York Times* described as "strips of buckskin across the knuckles." The gloves, real or imaginary, were important to this ruse because they supposedly brought Gilmore's boxing lectures within the new rules written in London by the Marquis of Queensberry, who insisted on three-minute rounds, a twenty-four-foot ring, and the wearing of gloves. Thus, any reasonable man might argue, if the professors wore gloves, they could hardly be accused of indulging in "a contention with fists."

There wasn't much Gilmore could do when his lease ran out in 1878, though. So, like Barnum, he abdicated in favor of a new

. . . and evangelists like Dwight L. Moody (top) and Ira D. Sankey occupy the pulpits and lead the revival meetings with spell-binding oratory.

Sometimes, Sankey sits and listens while Moody preaches. But everybody listens when the impresario Barnum takes the stage with his wild animals and acrobats and the exotic freaks and dancers who form the cast of "the Greatest Show on Earth."

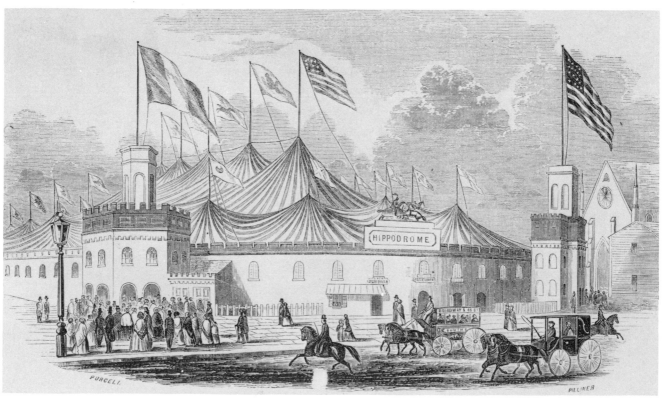

impresario, W. M. Tileston, an executive of the dog show, who added his own tone to things: a riding school, an archery range, lawn tennis, and an ice carnival.

But from waltzing elephants to waltzing boxers, the day of the sideshow was hurrying to its close. Commodore Vanderbilt had died the year before, and the empire passed to his son William, who promptly elected to reassert the family's control of its old railroad properties on Madison Square. The main event was about to begin.

The policy, William Vanderbilt said, would be to continue the dog show, the circus, and other "specials" as tenants of the arena. But the old railroad shed would operate principally in the future as an athletic center. Standing in the wings to give it life were two of the greatest attractions in sight, the National Horse Show, which figured to draw high society to the place, and John L. Sullivan, who figured to draw everybody else.

And on Memorial Day in 1879, with the curtain rising the next day, May 31, he even supplied a new name for his stage—Madison Square Garden.

The flags of the Congress of Nations flap in the breeze outside while cowboys chase Indians inside. And from waltzing elephants to waltzing boxers, the stage is set—from the Grand Roman Hippodrome to Gilmore's Garden to Madison Square Garden.

2 THE HORSEY SET

2

For New York's smart set in the late decades of the nineteenth century, the place to eat, meet and promenade is along Madison Square, where Fifth Avenue and Broadway cross Twenty-third Street. The landmarks include the Fifth Avenue Hotel; the finery includes bonnets and derby hats.

To Charles Dickens, who first visited the United States in 1842, America seemed a crude and tumultuous place where the people "ate piles of indigestible matter." By the time Dickens made his second visit in 1867, things had improved. At a dinner in honor of the celebrated English author, Delmonico's offered the following items of interest on its menu:

Among the *hors d'oeuvres chauds, timbales à la Dickens;* among the *poissons, saumon à la Victoria* or *bass à l'italienne* with *pommes de terre Nelson;* among the *relevés, agneau farci à la Walter Scott;* and among the *entrées, petits pois à l'anglaise* and *côtelettes de grouses à la Fenimore Cooper.* The decorations included such creations as *Temple de la Littérature, Les Armes Britanniques, Pavillon International, Colonne Triomphale,* and, for the local horsey set, *The Stars and Stripes.*

By then New York was drawing clear of the riotous street scenes of the Civil War and was growing into a seaport of nearly a million persons with a distinct turn toward what might be called culture. Or, to put it more directly, money.

The city already was becoming the home of the new aristocrats, as well as the target of the new international celebrities. The Swedish singer Jenny Lind, the thirty-year-old blond nightingale, was imported by P. T. Barnum with such fanfare that twenty thousand ardent admirers thronged the pier to witness her arrival. A few of them even fell off the pier in the crush. When Miss Lind made her debut at Castle Garden on the Battery at the lower tip of Manhattan, beneath a newly constructed roof, she was greeted by a crowd of six thousand persons who had

At the crossroads of American culture, international stars gather, too, starting with the Swedish singer Jenny Lind. She is imported by Barnum and lionized by throngs who pay as much as $225 a ticket.

Opposite:
But not many stars match the intrigue of Lola Montez, born Eliza Gilbert, endowed by the King of Bavaria and cheered as a *femme fatale* along "culture row."

paid as much as $225 for a ticket on the black market, an absolutely sure sign that culture had established a beachhead on New York's shores.

Another imported star was Albert Edward, Prince of Wales, who took up residence in the Fifth Avenue Hotel and was introduced to the city's society at an awesome ball held at the Academy of Music. Culture broke out there, too, when a horde of curious invaders stampeded the buffet dinner in his honor catered by Delmonico's, prompting John Jacob Astor III to organize a group of vigilantes to guard the door and the prince from further affronts.

Then there was Lola Montez, who advanced from the corps de ballet of a Paris theater into the arms and favor of the king of Bavaria, Ludwig I, an elderly patron of the arts, who gave her the title of Countess of Lansfeld as well as a voice in the affairs of state. That is, he did until he was forced to abdicate, after which Lola was forced to abdicate, too. But she simply joined the rush of culture to New York, where she promptly filled the Broadway Theater at twice the customary price for tickets.

Her specialty there was dancing, though she followed that success with an appearance as an actress in a play that was billed with historical tone as *Lola Montez in Bavaria*. After that she gave lectures on beauty, love, and European politics while living more or less serenely on West Seventeenth Street, not far from the heart of Manhattan's new "culture row." When she died at the age of forty-three, her role as a temptress was duly overshadowed by her role as an artiste; her gravestone in Greenwood Cemetery carried only the name Eliza Gilbert.

On the same stage of the Broadway Theater where Lola had glided, the great tragedian Edwin Forrest also delivered culture to the masses. And, not to be outdone by Lola, he also delivered some of the juiciest hours of personal scandal to the masses while handling eighteen major roles, from Macbeth and Hamlet to Othello and Richard III.

The scandal stemmed from a feud that Forrest fought with the English actor William Charles Macready, a feud so ferocious that gangs of toughs descended on the Astor Place Opera House to drive Macready from the stage. It was a bad moment for the development of art in New York. In the ensuing riot, the Seventh Regiment opened fire on the mob, killing twenty-two persons and injuring many more.

Where the Madison Cottage stood at mid-century, the Fifth Avenue Hotel opens its doors in 1859 and becomes the heart of life along the Square with its Amen Corner, "refined cuisine" and "scientific ventilation." For two bedrooms and a parlor: $30 a day.

FIFTH AVENUE HOTEL, MADISON SQUARE, NEW YORK,

HAS

A World-Wide Reputation

For its
Refined Cuisine,
For its
Convenient Situation,
For its
Scientific Ventilation,
For
Everything a Traveler needs.

Each corridor has an Iron Fire Escape from top to bottom.

Darling, Griswold, and Company, Proprietors.

This is also the world of dramatic acting, and for thirty years it is ruled by Edwin Booth, who portrays Hamlet in 1876 in a theater district that is far from melancholy.

As if all that weren't enough, Forrest then accused his wife of infidelity and sued her for divorce. He also turned on his old friend Nathaniel P. Willis, editor of the magazine *Home Journal*, and for good measure horsewhipped him in Washington Square. Finally, in the passion of the times, Forrest got into the habit of mixing curtain calls on stage with speeches denouncing both his wife and Willis.

In the same tradition, but without the same set of public outrages, Edwin Booth next took charge of the city stage and held it for thirty years as America's foremost actor. He brought Shakespeare to life with dramatic flourishes and a memorably rich voice, starting at the tender age of twenty-four and continuing for a generation and more, while New York acquired more fervor for the performing arts, more money to sponsor them, and more stages to hold them.

By the final third of the nineteenth century, as a result of such élan, actors were frequently lionized onstage but just as frequently ostracized offstage. They were pelted with flowers during curtain calls, swamped with attention at the stage doors, and eulogized by the column in the city's newspapers. However, when the actor George Holland died, the rector of a fashionable church on Fifth Avenue refused to open his sanctuary for the funeral of a mere "player," and suggested instead that the mourners try "the little church around the corner." That was the Church of the Transfiguration, on Twenty-ninth Street off Fifth Avenue, and the public responded to the slight with such aroused feeling that the Little Church Around The Corner was still famous as a haven for the theatrical set a century later.

"It is amazing how people spend their money," James Fenimore Cooper complained as the tide of the arts swept into town. "Twenty or thirty dollars to hear Jenny Lind are paid by those who live from hand to mouth. I cannot consent to pay thirty dollars for a concert, and they are welcome to their ecstasies."

Ecstasies, indeed. But the flow of cash proved as unpredictable as the flow of talent. When the young impresario Augustin Daly acquired the ramshackle old Broadway Theater near Thirtieth Street, he paid $14,000 in rent for the first year and then paid John Drew $30 a week to perform in it.

Even then, Drew took no chances, but wrote to his prospective employer as follows:

> My dear Mr. Daly:
> I beg to say that I will accept your offer of $30 or $35 per week for next season. Hoping sincerely that it may be in your power—as I am sure it is your inclination—to make it the latter. I remain, very sincerely, John Drew.

It was possible that John Drew addressed Daly with such deference, despite his own ranking in the theater, because Daly already had taken a leading role in the social life that was gathering around New York society in the late years of the nineteenth century. He was spending sums like $14,000 for rent and $30 for talent in 1879 for a clear purpose: reopening the Broad-

The passion offstage frequently rivals the passion onstage, as it does in the case of William Charles Macready, the English actor. He is even driven from the Astor Place Opera House by a gang of toughs during a feud with Edwin Forrest, the celebrated tragedian.

way Theater and making it the center of the city's new cultural life and the successor to such earlier showplaces as the Park Theater, Wallack's Theater, and the One Hundred and Sixty-fifth Street Theater.

His tastes were as varied as his audiences, too. At one end of the range of talent, he introduced performers like Ada Rehan (who got a flat offer of $35 a week), Fanny Davenport, Agnes Ethel, George Clarke, John Drew, and other emerging stars. At the other, way-out end of the range of talent, he imported a cluster of dancers and magicians from India, who arrived with exotic attractions that would have made even Barnum envious

—cobras. The manager of the troupe wrote to Daly while the caravan was en route to New York:

> They are enjoying the voyage, as healthy as possible under the circumstances, snuggled in a bag which is snuggled in a box. I hope some Customs Officer will put his hand in there. I think he will pass the rest of the chests.

To some people, the appearance of cobras would not have clashed radically with the physical environment surrounding the city's social and sporting growth. Manhattan was still stretching its civilization to the north from the tip of the island, and wide-open areas extended beyond the town houses, theaters, restaurants, and hotels downtown. The Upper West Side was still undeveloped and almost unknown, and a few farms still existed in midtown opposite the fancy new hotels that were inducing some well-heeled citizens to abandon housekeeping for the comforts of life at the inn.

Down near City Hall, there was the Astor House with its celebrated rotunda restaurant, a gathering place for the politicians and judges. Nearby were French's Hotel, Nash and Crooks, Lovejoys, and the United States, at Pearl and Fulton streets. McNells, on Greenwich Street, was close to the produce markets; the Cosmopolitan, on Chambers, stood conveniently close to the boats for Boston.

At Canal and Centre streets, there was Earle's Hotel; at Prince and Broadway, the brownstone Metropolitan. There were the St. Nicholas at Waverly Place, the Sinclair House at Eighth Street, and the St. Denis at Eleventh and Broadway, where the menu and the "Ladies' Mile" of fashionable stores attracted swarms of shoppers to the area.

At Union Square, the Morton House became an oasis for the actors who were leading the charge into the arts; the Clarendon still remembered that its earlier guests had included Thackeray and the Prince of Wales; and the Westminster boasted a guest list headed by Charles Dickens himself. At Fifth Avenue and Eighth Street stood the Brevoort (where it still stood a century later) and, at Twenty-third Street, the Fifth Avenue Hotel, which doubled as the headquarters of the Republican party in New York and which had a recess off the lobby known then (and generations later) as the Amen Corner, presumably because the party faithful headed there to say "amen" to party policy.

In the temper of the times, Edwin Forrest performs eighteen major roles, from Macbeth to Othello. But some of his strongest performances come during bitter speeches that embroil his private life with his curtain calls.

The farther north you traveled, the farther you were likely to travel up the social ladder. While it cost $30 a day for two bedrooms and a parlor at the Fifth Avenue Hotel, which was tony enough, there was a pronounced rise in luxury if not in price to the north, where the trees and the greenery of Madison Square created a setting of ultimate grace.

At Fifth and Twenty-sixth, the Brunswick Hotel was already becoming the official watering hole of the town's bankroll set, which flocked to the hotel en masse before and after the springtime and autumn parades of the Coaching Club. Across the street, Delmonico's restaurant created feasts that drew the famous in force. And nearby were the twin marble palaces, the Albemarle and the Hoffman House, the latter with its world-renowned bar festooned with murals of nude beauties painted by the Parisian artist Adolphe William Bouguereau.

The continental mood was continued at Twenty-seventh Street by the Victoria Hotel, resplendent in the French style and favored by President Grover Cleveland in later years whenever he visited New York. The mood changed somewhat to the East, where Madison Avenue and Fourth (or Park) Avenue provided the north-south routes for the horse-drawn carriages and where out-of-town horsemen and other sporting types were housed in less ornate places like the Ashland House and the Putnam House.

The hotels often reflected New York's mix of public life—political, social, and sporting. The Oriental, at Thirty-ninth Street, drew the theater crowd. The Gedney House, at Fortieth, catered to heroes of the prize ring like Tom Sharkey and Charlie Mitchell. And the Vanderbilt, at Forty-second and Lexington, became the headquarters of the one and only John L. Sullivan.

There was plenty of action in all these temples, whether it took the form of sumptuous free buffet lunches at the Hoffman bar, Roman banquets at Charles Delmonico's elegant restaurant, or a murder of passion at the Grand Central Hotel.

The murder of passion that most completely caught the imagination of the multitude starred Jim Fisk, the fat Romeo and finagling Wall Street partner of Jay Gould. The prize was Mrs. Helen Josephine Mansfield Salor, a comely divorcee from Boston who served as Fisk's "hostess" in a handsome brownstone behind the Grand Opera House on Twenty-third Street between Eighth and Ninth avenues. The "other man" was Edward S. Stokes, the free-spending son of a prominent New York clan, who was allied with Fisk in some questionable business deals but who was outraged at Fisk's attentions to Josie.

Fisk and Gould controlled the Erie Railroad, no question about that; but whether it was Fisk or Stokes who controlled Josie Mansfield was a considerable question. Then the financial scandals of the railroad threatened to become entwined with the after-hours scandals of Fisk, Stokes, and Josie. With lawsuits and exposures hanging over their heads, the principals played out a violent solution on the staircase of the Grand Central Hotel.

Passion also rules politics as private affairs mix scandalously with public affairs. Topping the list is Jim Fisk, the finagling Wall Street partner of Jay Gould and the portly suitor of Josie Mansfield, whose beauty proves fatal—to Fisk.

Fisk pays the price on the staircase of the Grand Central Hotel: two shots, fired point-blank by Edward S. Stokes, his rival for Josie. And as he lies dying in a room in the hotel, Fisk identifies his assassin: "There stands the man who shot me."

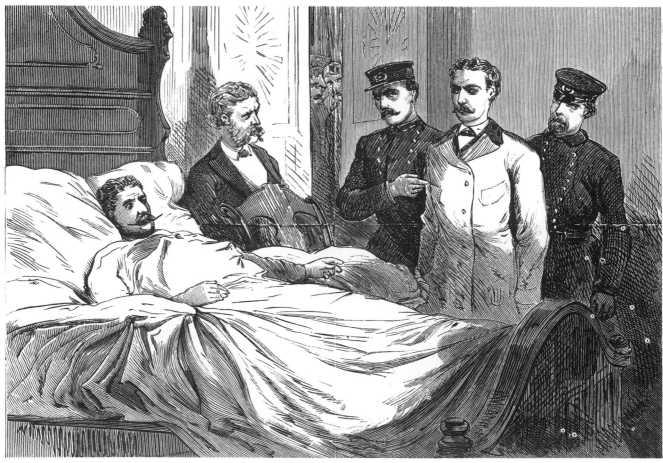

Stokes, the free-spending son of a prominent New York family, pays the price too: guilty of murder. Meanwhile, Jay Gould sheds tears—crocodile tears, some people suspect—over the body of his longtime crony and fellow manipulator of the Erie Railroad.

Fisk was striding up the long flight of stairs to the second floor one afternoon when he glanced up and saw Ned Stokes blocking his path with a pistol. Stokes fired twice at point-blank range, and Fisk toppled down the stairs. As he lay dying in a room in the hotel, he was visited by Gould, "Boss" Tweed, and an army of lawyers and doctors. After the funeral, *Harper's Weekly* ran a cartoon by Thomas Nast that depicted Gould and Tweed mourning at the grave and Gould saying, "All the sins of the Erie lie buried here."

But, in the spirit of the times, New York was able to forgive even if it could not forget. Fisk's body lay in state in the foyer of the Grand Opera House while the mourners and the curious filed by and the Ninth Regiment band supplied the dirges.

For sheer rollicking brass, though, nothing surpassed William Marcy Tweed himself. As the power behind the throne of Tammany Hall politics, as a state senator, and as the Boss of New York City, he masterminded things with flair and without fear. One week before the city election of 1870, the Boss treated his fellow citizens to "the works." A stupendous parade of 50,000 Democratic district workers wound along Broadway carrying flaming torches and signs of Tweed's favorite symbol, the tiger. President Grant sent two warships and two regiments to patrol the election, but they were no match for the Boss and his grip on the public purse and polls.

One thing was sure, the Boss was no piker. At the end of the Civil War, he had been bankrupt; eight years later, he owned a mansion at Madison Avenue and Fifty-ninth Street, a yacht, and a collection of immense diamonds, that he wore on his watch chain, his shirtfront, and several of his fingers. What caused his remarkable change in fortune? Some answers were supplied by George Jones, the editor of the *New York Times,* and by Thomas Nast, who drew his first "Tammany Tiger" cartoon for *Harper's Weekly* on November 11, 1871.

Jones, in his answer to the question, threw a searchlight on the Tweed Ring and its version of "honest graft," which was corrupting the city in the same way that the new art and architecture were enriching it. He found that Tweed, a onetime cabinetmaker, had stocked the city's armories with phantom chairs and phantom services costing one million dollars. The carpentry bill to New York came to $431,164. And the Boss's tab for plastering in the new county courthouse came to $2,870,000.

But the power behind the throne, and behind many of the public plots of the day, is the tiger of Tammany Hall, William Marcy Tweed: the Boss.

The *Times* kept challenging Tweed to submit to a public investigation of the city's finances, with the comptroller doing the investigating. Instead, Tweed named a six-man panel of citizens, including John Jacob Astor III, and they began to burrow into the accusations. Their conclusion: "The financial affairs of the city under the charge of the comptroller are administered in a correct and faithful manner."

The committee's sense of timing proved a lot sharper than its sense of history, however. The report was made public just

before election day. But George Jones and other reformers continued hammering away, and considerably less cheerful facts began to trickle out. Cuspidors for the city council's chamber, for example, were being billed at $190 apiece. Police jobs and transfers were sold from $300 to as high as $15,000 (captain,

The Tweed ring, after milking the city of millions, is finally dispersed after some relentless campaigning by the public press. A leading role in the overthrow is played by Thomas Nast, the political cartoonist, who depicts the Boss standing "on my record" in *Harper's Weekly*.

midtown). The comptroller, Richard B. Connolly, the man who supposedly held the civic purse strings, was universally known as "Slippery Dick." The city council was appropriately named "the Forty Thieves."

When Tweed finally was confronted with the goods, he was convicted in the same unplastered county courthouse that had cost the taxpayers $12 million and that already ranked as the most expensive public building in the United States, which may have been another sign of New York's rise as a city. He was still the old irrepressible Boss, though. He got off with a sentence of twelve months in jail and a fine of $12,500, a literal drop in the bucket of municipal finance. He served the twelve months and paid only $250, but meanwhile $500,000 was paid in fees to the lawyers who had arranged the "solution."

This was in 1873, the year when cable cars were being installed for the first time on the steep streets of San Francisco, nearly 3,000 miles west. Across the world, a supercool science student named Sherlock Holmes was embarking for the first time, as far as anybody could deduce, on a case where the game was afoot, "The Gloria Scott." And in the hamlet of Truxton in the Finger Lakes region of New York State, it was the year of the birth of John Joseph McGraw, who would reach New York City thirty years later as a baseball manager who for thirty years afterwards would lead the Giants to roaring success by day and lead an army of actors, jockeys, and celebrities to roaring entertainment by night.

It was also the year when P. T. Barnum leased Commodore Vanderbilt's abandoned railroad depot on Madison Square and began building his great elliptical arena there. Indeed, by then Barnum was already one of the impresarios of public entertainment in a city that was blossoming into a kind of social Renaissance, with new buildings that reached upward instead of outward and with a growing taste for leisure—all far from the disappearing buffalo herds of the country's disappearing frontier.

For years Barnum ran the show from his home at 484 Fifth Avenue, and he was a familiar figure around town. At the behest of Washington Irving, he headed the first industrial exhibition in the country, the Crystal Palace in Bryant Park. And he also served on the committee that created Central Park, with Irving as president of the commission.

Manhattan was still largely an island of horses drawing carriages by summer and sleds by winter, of people pedaling high-wheeled bicycles or sculling and rowing along the rivers, of buildings beginning to climb above the five floors of the Equitable headquarters. By 1870 the Tribune Building reached 285 feet, and eighteen years later, the Tower Building soared to thirteen floors, though it would be a dozen years more before the Park Row Business Building rose incredibly to twenty-nine stories above the streets of downtown New York, thanks to Otis and his new elevator of 1889.

By 1876 Central Park was basically laid out, with its lakes and reservoirs and carriage drives and its half-million plants and trees. Chinese immigrant families were beginning to settle in the neighborhood of Mott and Pell streets, while Italian restaurants were appearing on the fringe of Washington Square and German wine cellars were appearing at Union Square. In 1879 a twenty-three-year-old German named August Lüchow debarked in New York, and within three years he bought out the beer halls of his employer near Union Square, which had its own little culture corner that included Steinway Hall and the Academy of Music.

Somehow New York survives its "honest graft" and its political scandals and grows, upward and outward, while the country's population soars from 50 million to 75 million in one tumultuous generation.

For the average factory or shop worker, who went to work at 6:30 or 7:00 o'clock in the morning, these were off-limits places frequented mainly by the better-fixed, and so were the men's clubs that by now were sprouting around town.

The clubs were sprouting because society was becoming stratified, and rank had its privileges. Also its foibles, as Cleveland Amory noted many years later in *Who Killed Society*, a report on the strange and "beautiful" people who inherited the earth more frequently than the meek.

"The Century," he reported, etching the growth of club life in New York, "was formed in the belief that the Union was slighting intellectual eminence. 'There's a club down on Forty-third Street,' said one Union Clubber, 'that chooses its members mentally. Now, isn't that a hell of a way to run a club?'"

It may have been a hell of a way to run a club, but others were created for even more pointed reasons, to wit:

The Union League, a Republican club dating from 1863, was formed in answer to the fact that a Confederate Secretary of State was allowed to resign from the Union Club when, according to Union leaders, he should have been expelled. The Manhattan,

originally a Democratic club, was formed a year later in answer to the answer.

The Knickerbocker (1871) was formed because its members felt the Union was taking too many out-of-towners and wanted a club limited to men of Knickerbocker ancestry. The Metropolitan (1891) was formed because the elder J. P. Morgan could not get a friend of his into the Union, and thereupon, in the Morgan manner, built his own club.

The Brook (1903) was formed because two young Union Clubbers had been expelled for having attempted, unsuccessfully, upon the bald head of the Union's most revered patriarch, to poach an egg.

The predilections of society, whether for fame or fun, were mirrored to the masses through the pages of the newspapers and magazines, especially the new illustrated periodicals that were bringing a tone of their own to the arts-and-letters scene. There was the *Century*, founded by Roswell Smith and fortified by rewarding features like wood engravings and advertisements. There was *Harper's*, which, like the *Century*, sold for thirty-five cents a copy. And, before long, there was *Scribner's*, at twenty-five cents, followed by S. S. McClure's new magazine at only fifteen cents and, a few years later, Frank Munsey's publications at a rock-bottom ten cents.

If there was a geographical center for the city's burgeoning public life, it was the oasis of trees, mansions, and fine hotels surrounding Madison Square. To the south, down Broadway, stretched the "Ladies' Mile" of fashion, anchored by large and ornate new department stores like A. T. Stewart & Company, James McCreery & Company, Arnold Constable, and Lord & Taylor, plus dozens of small, chic shops. To the north and south, stylish hotels fringed the park. To the west, one block away but a world distant, Sixth Avenue roared with a kind of underworld of saloons and dance halls and finally an elevated railway that blackened the street below. And to the east, where Second and Third avenues dwindled toward the river, was a chaotic mix of everything else.

But if there was a cultural center for the city's new public life, it resided in a series of institutions that opened within a few years' time of one another: the Metropolitan Museum of Art in 1870, Madison Square Garden in 1879, the Metropolitan Opera House in 1883, and Carnegie Hall in 1891. There, on most

Madison Square grows, too. Along its avenues pass the state funerals for Abraham Lincoln and Ulysses S. Grant, the parades of the Tammany tigers, the processions of the circus elephants—and, in 1876, the torchlight celebration of the nation's Centennial.

William H. Vanderbilt, the son of Commodore Vanderbilt, helps lead an aristocrats' revolt that creates the Metropolitan Opera. And in 1879 he reclaims the family's old railroad depot and opens the doors to Madison Square Garden.

evenings of the year, the newly rich and the not-so-rich found common ground in uncommon settings.

However, in each case, culture came only after a lot of straining. The art museum, for example, had been a goal of New Yorkers like John Jay since the last decade of the previous century. But it wasn't until 1870 that the Metropolitan Museum was formed under the aegis of John Taylor Johnston, who had built the city's first marble mansion at Fifth Avenue and Eighth Street and who kept his own collection of paintings in a gallery above the stable.

Johnston and his colleagues had neither a museum nor an art

collection when they created the Metropolitan. But they met that problem two years later by buying 174 paintings in Europe, despite outcries against their "extravagance," and housed them in a rented brownstone on Fifth Avenue near Fifty-third Street.

It still took a great deal of public debate, petitions, and political pull with Boss Tweed before a permanent home for the museum was authorized. The site was along Fifth Avenue between Seventy-ninth and Eighty-fourth streets, where Central Park was reaching north toward Harlem. However, the museum shifted around town for years until its new home was ready—from Dodsworth's Dance Hall at 681 Fifth Avenue to the Douglas Mansion on Fourteenth Street near Sixth Avenue, later the address of a Salvation Army storehouse.

Johnston, who used to allow the public into his private gallery, subscribed $10,000 to get things moving. But even after the doors were opened uptown, he and the trustees were berated for keeping the museum closed on Sundays, the one day the man in the street presumably had free from his workweek to absorb a little culture. The crusade for Sunday hours was led by J. A. Mitchell, the editor of *Life* magazine, and Charles Dana Gibson, the artist, who later reached the man in the street himself by creating the celebrated "Gibson girls." And, after years of bickering, the man in the street got his culture on Sunday.

The same sort of infighting and jockeying marked the founding of the Metropolitan Opera. One of the issues was that the Academy of Music had space for only eighteen boxes for the city's royal families, and it was said that not even $30,000 could pry one loose.

The solution, obviously, was to build your own opera house and nail down your own royal box, the way J. P. Morgan had got the ball rolling for the Metropolitan Club. Armed with this theory, the Vanderbilt family took the lead in organizing the group that deserted the old Academy on Fourteenth Street and migrated to the new opera temple on Thirty-ninth. They got their royal boxes, all right; tier upon tier, with names like the Diamond Horseshoe and the Golden Horseshoe, horsey places indeed and miles below the upper reaches of the balcony known as the Family Circle.

They also got a deficit of half a million dollars. But the battle was won. Within two years, in the spring of 1885, the Academy of Music surrendered, closing its doors while Col. James H. Ma-

First Annual N. Y.

Bench Show.

CATALOGUE

1877.

NEW YORK:
ROGERS & SHERWOOD, PRINTERS, 21 BARCLAY STREET.
1877.

As the Garden takes over the social and sporting scene of the park, it inherits Barnum's circus and one other tenant: the dog show. They will become the longest-running shows in town.

pleson, the impresario there, lamented, "I cannot fight Wall Street."

While all this was going on, something was also stirring down on Madison Square, and the Vanderbilts were the prime movers there, too.

The Commodore's son, William, was reclaiming control of the old railroad shed and the adjoining properties, where Barnum's elephants had waltzed and Barnum's chariots had raced in the days of the Monster Classical and Geological Hippodrome, where Gilmore had staged his boxing "exhibitions," and where Dwight Moody had led his revival meetings.

This was where the city's social and sporting life flowed together, in the theaters of the Rialto, the shops of the "Ladies' Mile," the great mahogany bars of the elegant hotels where John L. Sullivan reigned, and the plush dining rooms of Delmonico's and the other ornate restaurants where society herded itself in old New York.

This was where the great parades and rallies were staged and where New York said goodby to its heroes in memorable funeral processions: General William J. Worth, one of the city's celebrities of the War of 1812 and the Mexican War, Abraham Lincoln, Horace Greeley, and later, Ulysses S. Grant.

"In all of New York," observed a historical sketch of the day, "there is no other one place so completely identified with the growth of the city as this beautiful pleasance. It is doubtful if there is any place in the world where the *fin de siècle* civilization in its fullest development can be seen to greater advantage. It has all the gaiety and brightness of the famous Place de la Concorde in Paris. Like Trafalgar Square in London, it has a memorial to a nation's greatest naval hero. Its history is like that of Lafayette Square in Washington city. The history of Madison Square is indeed the history of New York city itself."

And there, on the day after Memorial Day in 1879, William Vanderbilt threw open the doors of Madison Square Garden, the biggest and newest stage in town, dedicating it to athletic excellence and inaugurating it, in the spirit of the upbeat times, with a concert that filled the Knickerbockers' old ball field with music.

3 GARDEN I
Goddesses

The date is May 31, 1879. The place: the northeast corner of Madison Square. The first Garden opens with a band concert featuring sixty musicians.

Decoration Day, they called it then. It was a hot, stifling Friday and the start of a holiday weekend that already seemed heavy with memorial services, reunions of veterans from the Grand Army, and speeches reviving the meaning and the memory and the massacre of Gettysburg.

A few special memories were being revived that weekend in Boston, where they were burying and praising William Lloyd Garrison, the old abolitionist, whom they once had chased down alleys with rope and noose. He escaped that time when the mayor of Boston sprang from his office in City Hall and wrested Garrison from the mob, just short of the Common, and then protected him inside the walls of the Leverett Street jail. But now on this holiday weekend in 1879, they came with eulogies, without bitterness, without rope.

Over in New Haven, the public passion was being spent in another way. A throng of 1,500 people turned out to watch Yale beat Brown, 2–0, in the first baseball game played between the two schools. On the next afternoon, a hot holiday Saturday, the Yalies did it again, this time beating Princeton, 3–0. All told, it may have been one of the best weekends on record for Yale pitching, whatever it was to other Americans.

To most other Americans, it was chiefly the time when winter finally surrendered to summer, with spring sandwiched in between. Under the heading "News by States" that weekend, the *New York Times* reported that Wisconsin was entering "the dust season for crops" while Nebraska was expecting "an enormous yield of cereals." In Michigan, "the most beautiful harvest

51

William Lloyd Garrison, once vilified because he favored an immediate end to slavery, is laid to rest in Boston on the same weekend that the Garden opens. Now, fifteen years after the Civil War, the old abolitionist is buried —with eulogies.

ever known is promised, and the cereals and fruits are doing well," while farther west in Minnesota, "the wheat crop is in splendid condition, with expectations of an increased yield of 30 per cent." And in the Indian Territory, not yet carved into states, the word was this:

"In the cattle regions, the grazing is finer than it has ever been, and a larger supply of cattle will be driven to market than usual."

The Forty-sixth Congress was sitting in Washington, but not that weekend. Its members headed for the country or, more likely, for the backyard. Or, if you happened to be one of their better-heeled constituents, you might be headed north from the sweltering streets of New York for a resort like Saratoga Springs, where the Grand Union Hotel had opened for business the year before with this advertising fanfare:

"The latest and most magnificent summer hotel in the world. Rooms can be secured on application at the Metropolitan Hotel, New York."

If, on the other hand, you stayed in town for the holiday, Arnold Constable was festooning its store at Broadway and Nineteenth Street with "Paris-made costumes, parasols and parasolettes, lace-trimmed, fringed, and embroidered." Or, over at A. T. Stewart & Co., a few blocks down Broadway between Ninth and Tenth streets, "ready-made suits, special bargains in misses' dresses, made of white piqué, percale, and linen." Or, for some really selective shopping, R. H. Macy & Co. was offering "black silks, at a special bargain, 99 cents per yard—good value for $1.35 per yard."

Over at the United States Custom House, a new auditor was just taking over his desk, and if it had included a nameplate, which it didn't, the sign would have read: Colonel Charles Treichel. Over at Association Hall, the last in a series of medical talks was concentrating on "voluntary diseases," whatever they were. Over at 14 Warren Street, the final entries were being received for "the 36-hour professional and the 24-hour amateur championship walking matches," whatever *they* were. And along the riverfront, the steamer *Faraday* was settling into its berth after a crossing from Liverpool during which, the captain reported, the ship had "passed large icebergs near Cape Race."

If the man of the house chose to stay close to the hearth this holiday weekend, a glance at the front page brought him news of "the campaign in Ohio," an analysis of "how Europe is governed," and details from Washington on "the Democrats backing down on appropriations." Also, since the violence of the weather always made headlines, this late word from landlocked Abilene:

> A terrible storm of wind and rain passed over northern Kansas and southern Nebraska last evening. The town of Irving, ninety miles west of St. Louis, was nearly destroyed. At that point, the storm took the character of a cyclone and leveled everything in its path. About forty buildings were destroyed and fifteen persons were killed, while thirty to forty were *wounded.*

To escape from the grimness of Page One, and perhaps to escape from the grimness of a sultry weekend in town, the housebound New Yorker might consider the message in the advertisement beneath the bold-faced, eye-catching heading: "Ho!" The rest of the ad told of the joy of riding the excursion trains on the Long Island Railroad: leaving from Long Island City and from the Bushwick and Flatbush Avenue Depot at the corner of Atlantic Avenue in Brooklyn at 9:00 o'clock and 11:30 in the morning on Sunday or even at 1:30 in the afternoon; returning from the beach at Far Rockaway, then a long haul down the tracks, at 3:00 or 4:30 or 5:30 in the afternoon. Tab for the round trip: 50 cents.

For a total escape from the inner-city scene, nothing compared with a day at the races. The only catch was that not many people had the time or the money to finance such an escape. Still, the dominant headline at the top of the right-hand side of the front page of the *Times* on that Saturday, May 31, read: "The Jockey Club Races. Opening of Jerome Park Spring Meeting. A Warm Day and a Small Attendance." And the lead paragraphs of the story told, in a chatty and narrative style, how life was treating the horsey set on this holiday weekend:

> The holiday people remained at home yesterday, and their absence diminished the attendance at Jerome Park by fully 8,000 as compared with the previous day. The falling-off was nearly as perceptible on the clubhouse bluff as on the grandstand and on Deadhead Hill, outside the fence. The latter eminence was thinly sprinkled with a bare thousand or so of the impecunious.

That's what the man said: "of the impecunious," meaning the freeloading spectators who tried to watch the races from the "eminence" outside the gates known as Deadhead Hill, the place where the "deadheads" presumably gathered.

Without troubling to soften the grandeur of its point of view, the report continued:

> Less than 500 expended 50 cents apiece for the privilege of sitting on the mound to the north of the grandstand. Three thousand would cover all of the occupants of the stand itself, and 1,500 would be a liberal allowance for the bluff.
> The Four-in-Hand Club made a fine display. There were no less than ten coaches drawn up in line in front of the clubhouse, and their luncheon parties whitened the grass along the slope.

In other words, a tailgate party in the horse-and-buggy era. Afterwards, the racetrack emptied and everybody headed back home for the rest of the Decoration Day weekend—the Four-

THE HERALD

Harrison
carries the
State by
12000.

in-Hand Club people in their ten coaches, their less affluent neighbors who had "expended" fifty cents apiece, and the impecunious thousand who had spent the afternoon outside the fence on Deadhead Hill. For some in the traffic streaming away from Jerome Park, there was still the long evening ahead unfolding in the theaters, restaurants, concert halls, and saloons of Manhattan.

Over at the Academy of Music, the cast was taking the stage for the evening's performance of Verdi's *Il Trovatore,* exactly a quarter century after its first performance in Rome. And over at Wallack's Theater, the cast was taking the stage for the final performance of Shakespeare's *As You Like It.*

Since this was the end of the week and also the end of the month, a kind of changing of the guard might customarily be taking place along theater row. But, as the *Times* noted in its Sunday edition, which was going to press that evening:

> Nothing new is planned at any theater except at Wallack's during the coming week, although those who are willing to be entertained in spite of these "rare June days" may fall back gracefully on the invincible "Pinafore" at the Standard. At Wallack's tomorrow evening, the fresh woodland beauty of "As You Like It" will fade, panorama-wise, into the artificial atmosphere of "The Hunchback."

That's what the man said: "panorama-wise," which may have made him an adventurer in the language that later would permeate Madison Avenue. In any event, panorama-wise, to borrow his phrase, the biggest group of nightlife devotees on that hot evening were headed for the tree-lined park known as Madison Square, which had been the center of New York entertainment since Barnum marched his elephants into the wooden stalls of Commodore Vanderbilt's old railroad shed.

The place was the same, but the act had changed down through the years of religious revivals led by Dwight Moody, flower shows, temperance meetings, policemen's balls, and the more recently inaugurated Westminster Kennel Show. The management had also changed; William Vanderbilt was now wearing the hat of chief impresario with a policy of converting the complex into an athletic center. On this night, he rang up the curtain on the new athletic center with a very nonathletic opening event, a concert, perhaps out of deference to the holiday or the heat, perhaps out of deference to the fact that Patrick

Sarsfield Gilmore, the most recent resident genius, was a celebrated bandmaster.

Whatever the reason, the crowd was there and so was the music, and the *Times* recorded the occasion in these words under an unmistakably clear and succinct headline:

MADISON SQUARE GARDEN

"Gilmore's Garden," under its new name, was opened last night for the first of a series of summer-night concerts, Mr. Harvey B. Dodworth being the musical director, with a band of some sixty performers.

The Garden has been fitted up with all the appliances for the enjoyment of visitors, and presented a brilliant spectacle last night. An immense audience was present, the boxes and seats along the sides being fully occupied, while the seats in the body of the building and the promenade were crowded.

It is the purpose of the management to give concerts nightly, the programmes of which will be of a popular character, and suited to the demands of most pleasure-seekers, who do not wish to be called on for any serious mental effort while taking their amusements.

The band is full and efficient, and up to the highest standards of similar bands heard before in the same place. The selections last night comprised overtures, waltzes and potpourris, and solos for the cornet.

Mr. Dodworth has several excellent solo performers engaged for the season, some of whom are well known and others, like Signor Liberati, who have come to New York with high professional reputations.

The opening night was certainly a great success and, despite the excessive heat, the concert was evidently enjoyed by the thousands in attendance.

The thousands in attendance—that was the glory of the Garden and, before long, the problem of the Garden: *keeping* the thousands in attendance. Gilmore had tried it with a wide-ranging series of shows, including—one year to the night before Madison Square Garden opened—something called "a testimonial benefit tendered to I. M. Laflin, the champion club-swinger and inventor of the parlor rowing apparatus."

There was nothing wrong with that, not for one night anyway. But how many people would keep paying to benefit the champion club-swinger of New York, even in the city's Victorian Age of rousing entertainment? The answer, William Vanderbilt discovered fast, was: not enough.

To meet the problem, only three years after opening the doors, Vanderbilt turned to the one sure thing needed to enable his showplace to compete with the attractions then being offered on almost every block of midtown Manhattan—a star. And the brightest star in town was John L. Sullivan, the 195-pounder who had begun fighting the year before the Garden's first-night concert and who won the heavyweight title on February 7, 1882,

The first hero and attraction in the Garden is John L. Sullivan, "the Boston Strong Boy," who becomes heavyweight champion in 1882. Boxing is periodically outlawed as a barbaric event, but for years John L. reigns in the Garden through a series of sellout "exhibitions."

by knocking out Paddy Ryan in the ninth round of a bareknuckle bout in Mississippi City.

Five months later, on July 17, the Garden installed Sullivan as its main event. He went four rounds against a British heavyweight known as Tug Wilson, sometimes also known as Joe Collins, who survived the champion's standing offer: any man still standing after four rounds with John L. would get $1,000 and half the gate receipts. It was a lackadaisical fight but a financial coup: the place was jammed, and 10,000 people were turned back from the doors before they were closed and locked for the evening.

The presence of Sullivan in the Garden also served another purpose: It gave some respectability to boxing, which was considered a rowdy pastime at best and the devil's own work at worst. Even serious newspapers like the *New York Times* began to cover the fights, and not just because they drew almost as many policemen as customers. But, whatever they drew, they drew attention, especially on the night of May 14, 1883, when Sullivan was knocked down by Charlie Mitchell in the first round before a crowd that the press described in terms of elegant gear: "silver-headed walking sticks, opera hats, white shirt fronts and evening ulsters."

To add some spice to the program, Sullivan got up off the floor and took after Mitchell, who was the British heavyweight champion. By the third round, John L. had the upper hand; and, by the third round, the police made their customary invasion of the hall, stopping the fight, the captain later reported, "just short of murder."

One year later, the constables not only halted the fight but also arrested Sullivan in the second round of his bout with Al Greenfield for "outraging decency and tending to corrupt public morals." And the year after that, early in 1885, they broke up a return match between Sullivan and Paddy Ryan less than a minute after it had started before a crowd of 11,000. After that, Sullivan's reign as the star of the show faded fast, and the Garden hunted unhappily for other drawing cards.

Sometimes the drawing cards were singers; sometimes they were dancers or acrobats; sometimes show dogs and jumping horses. On the night of November 21, 1888, they were men in track suits.

It was a bitterly cold night, inside the arena as well as outside

One of his legendary opponents is the English champion, Charlie Mitchell, who even knocks Sullivan down in the first round. But by the third round, Mitchell is on the receiving end when the police stop the fight "just short of murder."

in Madison Square, but a capacity crowd showed up, and one report of the event said that "enthusiasm supplied the warmth which the furnaces failed to furnish." The enthusiasm was forced to survive a program of eighteen events billed as a national championship meet, and it did, largely because this was an indoor meet staged two months after the outdoor championships had been held in Detroit.

There wasn't much science or precision involved in the judging, but at least the cops didn't raid the joint. In the 150-yard dash, for example, the officials weren't sure who had crossed the line first, W. C. White of New York or S. J. King of Washington. They finally decided that King had finished "two inches behind," meaning that the New York sprinter had won the race. That may have been the first time that "the home-court advantage" was suspected in a Garden contest.

There were other peculiarities, too. The pole vault was decided by horizontal distance over the ground, not vertical distance over a bar. The 56-pound-weight throw, by contrast, was decided by height rather than distance. Somebody named M. O. Sullivan flung the weight 13 feet 11⅝ inches and somehow avoided being brained by his own toss.

But when all was said and done, the greatest star of the first Garden in the 1880s was neither a weight thrower nor a heavyweight, not even the legendary John L. Sullivan. It was the twenty-two-year-old African elephant named Jumbo, an international star, at that, who was imported onto the scene to the fanfare of trumpets by the pioneer showman of Madison Square Park, P. T. Barnum.

Thirty years earlier, Barnum had established himself as the master when he imported Jenny Lind from Stockholm, personally met her at the gangway of the S.S. *Atlantic* and escorted her in his private carriage from shipside at Canal Street to the Irving House on Broadway at Chambers Street. Ten minutes after their arrival at the hotel, a crowd of 20,000 persons thronged the street. And Barnum, building the suspense, let them throng the street all afternoon and evening before he led the Swedish nightingale to the balcony window at midnight and let her throw kisses to the raging public that he had created.

He displayed the same sense of showmanship for her debut at Castle Garden, where the first seats were auctioned off for $225 while sixty policemen patrolled the Battery, 6,000 customers filled the auditorium, and many others bobbed around in small boats offshore. Jenny responded by singing arias from operas, then brought Barnum onstage for her curtain calls, and pocketed $12,600 as her share of the purse.

During the next generation, New York developed its capacity for the public "spectacular," and people like Barnum made sure that it did. By the late 1870s, when the Garden was providing him with a properly dramatic stage for his imagination, the city surrounding the stage was providing him with the audience and the craving for diversion that made it all work.

It was a city in transition, and a lively transition at that. For people going places, ferryboats streamed across the East River in the shadow of the massive construction project that soon would produce the Brooklyn Bridge. Somewhat finer boats carried local travelers downtown along the East River from Harlem to the Battery. Along the avenues, which paralleled the river's north-south route, horses drew carriage cars; and, for ten cents extra, the more discriminating passenger on the Third Avenue line could ride the "drawing-room car." Crosstown traffic was often clogged on main arteries like Fulton Street, where the ferries from Brooklyn docked.

By night the streets still blinked in gaslight, but not for long. In a dingy office on Pearl Street, a man named Thomas Alva Edison was working on one of his dozens of inventions, a light that required neither match nor fuel. People tended to be amused by Edison and his eccentricities, but not for long either. At least, they sat up and took notice when the *New York Times* office, then at Park Row, got itself equipped with Edison's "electric light."

Over at the American Institute Fair, a man named Alexander Graham Bell was showing off *his* invention, and for ten cents you could try it out, talking from one end of the hall to the other, as Henry Collins Brown remembered years later:

> I squandered a dime for this and remember holding a hollow thin disk to my ear and speaking through it and hearing a voice from the other end. It attracted no attention and was considered on a par with the dozen other insignificant catch-penny devices which invariably accompanied any public exhibition of this sort.

A few days later, though, Bell gave a more formal and practical demonstration at Chickering Hall, and this time it did attract attention. According to the *Times,* this is what happened.

At Chickering Hall last evening before 300 persons, Professor Alexander Graham Bell lectured on the speaking telephone. At the end of the lecture, Professor Bell stated that he had intended to give what he believed would have been interesting and instructive illustrations of the power of the telephone, but unfortunately his improved instruments had not arrived from Boston and he would have to content himself with displaying a telephone of inferior power.

This was connected by an ordinary telegraph with an improved telephone in New Brunswick, New Jersey, thirty-two miles away and this, in turn, was attached to an ordinary organ, upon which a number of simple tunes would be played and the sounds transmitted to New York by means of his instruments.

He then telegraphed to New Brunswick and shortly after, from a little box on the stage, and from other instruments in different parts of the hall, came the music of the song known as "The Sweet Bye and Bye." This was followed by "Home, Sweet Home," and afterward by "Hold the Fort," sung by a strong baritone voice and plainly audible. After this, Professor Bell and Mr. C. W. Field asked a number of questions through the telephone. They were all answered satisfactorily by those at the end of the wire in New Brunswick.

When he wasn't forking over ten cents for a personal preview of the new age of marvels, the man in the street could entertain himself and his curiosity in a thousand other ways, depending on his personality and his pocketbook. There were rowing on the city's rivers, croquet in Central Park and Prospect Park, rifle shooting and archery, the new sport of football and the newly established sport of baseball, and boxing on the sly or even on river barges. *Harper's Weekly,* the final arbiter of sporting matters, reviewed the scene and issued a searching report:

Whether baseball is a better or a worse game than cricket, we do not now propose to inquire; but it is really worthwhile inquiring whether the former is or is not as popular among us as is commonly reported in the newspapers. In New York, it is well known that there are several baseball clubs which play periodically. The same thing is true of Boston, Philadelphia and perhaps one or two other cities. But is baseball so popular that it is a regular and well-understood diversion in most of the counties in most of the states of the Union?

We leave it to those who are better acquainted with the sporting fraternity than ourselves to answer these queries. For our part, we regret to say that we doubt very much whether baseball be a popular game at all in the interior, or in any part of the country except in a few great cities. We see no evidence that either baseball

This is the time when life is being transformed by a rush of inventions: the electric elevator, the Linotype machine, the internal-combustion engine. But the wizard is Thomas A. Edison, who creates (above) the first phonograph and who later presides over a laboratory that produces the electric light.

or any other athletic game is so generally practiced by our people as to be fairly called a popular American game.

Truxton, in upstate New York, did not rank then as one of the "few great cities," but one of its young citizens named John J. McGraw would have cheerfully punched the writer for *Harper's Weekly* in the snout. At sixteen, McGraw already was getting $5 every time he pitched for East Homer up in the David Harum country. Then he was hired by Olean in the New York and Pennsylvania League, also known as the Iron and Oil League, and began getting $40 a month plus room and board.

"Dad," he told his father, who was as doubting as *Harper's Weekly*, "I'll be making $3,500 a year before you know it."

As a result of all the changes in day-to-day life, and especially city life, people seemed to be growing remarkably ripe for enchantment of almost any kind. And nobody supplied enchantment with as much dash as Barnum.

He already was drawing great crowds to his museum at Broadway and Ann Street in lower Manhattan, where he had followed up his success with Jenny Lind by staging a running series of sensational attractions. There was, for example, Gen. Tom Thumb, the engaging midget. For an encore, under Barnum's aegis, the general was married off to dainty Miss Lavinia Warren. (To complete the fantasy, Miss Lavinia survived the museum and the general, too, and lived out her days in a magical sort of doll's house in Medford, Massachusetts, a folk hero straight from Barnum's Broadway.)

But from midgets to mammoths, no folk hero in Barnum's repertoire stood taller in the streets than Jumbo. He was intelligent and gentle, he was responsive and playful with children, he was already the ranking star of the London Zoo when Barnum bought him in 1882 for $10,000. He probably didn't need any further buildup, but Barnum provided one anyway by the simple act of putting up the purchase price.

The sale provoked a storm of protest that bordered on becoming an international incident. John Ruskin, the distinguished writer and art critic, complained publicly that England was not in the habit of parting with her national pets. Queen Victoria and the Prince of Wales, patrons of the Royal Zoological Society, which was Jumbo's home, also protested. Barnum was sued in Chancery Court, which not only injected more publicity into the situation but also upheld the American—at a price. The

Machines are not the only marvels of the age. From midgets to mammoths, the great Barnum dazzles the public with folk heroes, and one of his giant attractions is the tiny but engaging Gen. Tom Thumb.

price was precautionary, and that only added to the uproar; the court ruled that two entire decks of the ship must be cleared for the elephant's crossing from England to New York. Undaunted, Barnum paid $30,000 more for all the space that passengers would have bought on the two decks of the steamship *Assyrian Monarch*. Finally, while English children wept at the pier,

The surest sign of spring every year is the arrival of the circus, and Barnum makes certain that nobody misses the sign. He parades the whole show through town from the railroad yards to the destination, the Garden.

Jumbo was crated into an ironbound box that weighed more than twelve tons with him inside, and London lost a superstar.

The passage across the North Atlantic took fourteen days, which only increased the suspense. But on April 6, Jumbo and his keeper landed in New York. It took a floating derrick to unload the great elephant and then—another of Barnum's brainstorms—it took sixteen horses to pull Jumbo on a flatcar from the dock to Madison Square Garden, where Barnum's show was then on exhibit.

New York, much to the Garden's financial relief, went hysterical. Within three days of Jumbo's grand arrival as the star of the cast, Barnum had recovered every penny of the money he had spent to buy and import him. During the next four circus seasons, with two-a-day appearances around the country, Jumbo was shown to four million children and maybe four times that many adults. And when Jumbo died at the age of twenty-six, he went to two elephants' graveyards, where his legend was preserved: His skin was stuffed and mounted at Tufts College, and his skeleton was arrayed at the American Museum of Natural History.

Jumbo created another legacy too, which survived the arena on Madison Square where he had scored his greatest success: The march of the elephants through New York each year became the universal sign of the great traveling circus. And the opening of the circus at the Garden became the universal sign of spring.

Unfortunately, spring was followed by summer, fall, and winter, and on too many nights in those seasons, the Garden lacked both an act and a star. The management tried to keep the hall filled by scheduling flower shows, cattle sales, lectures on temperance, even masked balls and Elks conventions. But the winners were few and far between.

On many evenings the place was empty; on others, which was worse, it was cold and empty. They never had been able to heat the cavernous place very well, and now the same winter weather that once drove Barnum south was driving the customers away. Vanderbilt even tried to beat the elements one night by flooding the main floor and converting it into a colossal ice-

skating rink, but that didn't work either. A sudden thaw put an end to that scheme and led people to observe that the entire business was probably on thin ice, too.

Vanderbilt, who did not enjoy losing money, decided finally that enough was enough. The Garden, which was portrayed by *Harper's Weekly* as a "patched-up, grimy, drafty, combustible old shell," would have to be razed. His decision probably comforted the stockholders of the New York Central Railroad, the nucleus of his empire, but it didn't do much for the members of the Horse Show Association. They were charter members of the Garden too, and they had enough financial clout to do something about the impending loss of their favorite horse yard.

With James T. Woodward leading the way, they formed a syndicate that included some formidable pillars of New York society as well as some formidable bankrolls: Hiram Hitchcock, Frank Sturgis, William F. Wharton and, last but by no means least, John Pierpont Morgan.

Their purpose was simple: When Vanderbilt razed the Garden, they didn't want him to sell the site for a hotel, restaurant, department store, warehouse, or even church. They wanted to make certain that Madison Square would still be the home of Madison Square Garden, and a new and grander one at that. If that purpose seemed expensive, they were ready where it counted. In the summer of 1887, they raised $1,500,000 to finance the project and headed for the drawing board.

For the next two years the old Garden still operated with its flower shows, horse shows, Elks conventions, and even its new-fangled indoor track meet and the Democratic National Convention of 1888. But the place seemed emptier than ever without the magic of its first and foremost superstars, Jumbo and the great John L.

The day of Jumbo and the great John L. passes, but a new home for the old Garden is planned by a syndicate of wealthy New Yorkers led by captain of finance John Pierpont Morgan.

4 GARDEN II
Jumbo and John L.

"Madison Square Garden," observed *Harper's Weekly*, holding the mirror to New York life toward the close of the nineteenth century, "owing to its happy location and what may be termed the 'goodwill' of the spot, arising from the habit of citizens to go there for amusements of various kinds, has been marked these many years as the place for some building of public entertainment much finer than the present structure.

"It was determined to erect a composite edifice embracing a hippodrome, theatre, ballroom, restaurant, concert hall and summer garden, thus forming a sort of pleasure exchange or central palace of pleasure."

Happy location, indeed. Goodwill of the spot, for sure. The habit of citizens to go there for amusements of various kinds, no question about that.

It was a happy location for actors, athletes, politicians, and professional people, for the "swells" of the town, for star-crossed lovers like Jim Fisk and Josie Mansfield before Ned Stokes squeezed the trigger. It was the magnet that drew Lillian Russell on the arm of "Diamond Jim" Brady, two of the most celebrated and probably the best fed of the customers who swarmed to Delmonico's and Sherry's. It was restaurant row, hotel row, and theater row. And most of all, perhaps, it was the place where Stanford White lived and worked and, they say, loved.

Wherever the smart set went in New York, the comforts of life were graced in every direction by the talent, and frequently by the presence, of Stanford White, architect and *bon vivant*, the artistic leader of the renaissance that was endowing the city with new buildings, monuments, facades, and statues.

When the town fathers decided to erect a memorial to Adm.

The new Garden rises on the site of the old, its tower commanding the tree-lined park of Madison Square.

David Farragut, this being the age of heroes, they called in the sculptor Augustus Saint-Gaudens and Stanford White; and, this being the age of happy locations, they decided to place it in Madison Square. Saint-Gaudens did the statue and White designed the base. They did such a formidable job that they next were commissioned by the banker J. P. Morgan to design a tomb. Correct: a tomb.

When a tower was proposed for the Judson Memorial Church on Washington Square, opposite Washington Mews and MacDougal Alley and alongside elegant homes belonging to first families named Rhinelander, Van Rensselaer, and Stewart, the task was assigned to Stanford White. He responded by designing a classic structure in the Renaissance style that soon provided studio apartments for some of the most established artists in town.

When a group of society women blazed a trail of their own by founding the Colony Club, complete with a bar that touched off a furor in the press and pulpits of the city, they chose Madison Avenue as the site and Stanford White as the architect. When half a dozen millionaires migrated uptown and created a haven of magnificent homes, they selected an area on the fringe of Harlem that had nothing in common with the poor people's neighborhood nearby—and selected Stanford White as the architect.

When William C. Whitney purchased a mansion on Fifth Avenue at Sixty-seventh Street and later decided to refurbish the interior, he naturally commissioned Stanford White to handle the job. Just as naturally, the job took four years, because White, sparing neither his imagination nor Whitney's money, imported stained-glass windows from Europe, gates from Rome, a ballroom from a castle in France, and one entire corridor from a monastery in the French countryside.

When Mrs. Stuyvesant Fish converted her mansion on Madison Avenue at Seventy-eighth Street, she turned the conversion over to Stanford White. He rose to the occasion by creating what came to be known as "a palace of the doges," a showplace that included such incidentals as a lavish Gothic bedroom and a ballroom that came equipped with a 300-piece gold dinner service and, at festive times, brass bands, dance troupes, a modest circus, and a baby elephant.

When James Hazen Hyde decided to pitch a memorable ball

—memorable enough to surpass any other in memory—he consigned the details to Stanford White. The architect responded by reproducing the Hall of Mirrors at Versailles. He installed it in the ballroom of Sherry's restaurant and garnished it with thousands of orchids and mounds of caviar and diamondback terrapin. The tab, Hyde let it be known, came to $200,000.

As a result of such monuments to society's taste and wealth, as well as to White's inventiveness, it came as no surprise to people when Barnum's old circus barn was ruled off the map in 1887 in favor of a new "central palace of pleasure," the second Madison Square Garden. And it certainly came as no surprise that the design for the palace was entrusted to Stanford White.

He was allowed $75,000 as a commission to execute the task, and he promptly set the proper tone for the project by suggesting $450,000 more to add a tower. Just as promptly, the stock market hit the skids with such stunning force that the Garden's financial angels began to have second thoughts. Some suggested that it might be more prudent to build a department store on the site, or perhaps an apartment house that would return a more certain profit, or, to be absolutely certain, a post office.

But, after all, this was the golden age of both art and finance, and no time for the faint of heart. So John Pierpont Morgan, with his 3,000 shares of common stock in the venture, and Stanford White, with 1,000 shares, pooled their resources and prestige and rallied the other investors for the long haul. They succeeded, and in a style that did no damage to Morgan's reputation as a money man nor to White's reputation as a thinking man.

The wrecking crews began to demolish the old Garden in July of 1889, and during the next twelve months the new hippodrome rose among the shade trees on the New York Knickerbockers' old baseball field. It extended 200 feet on one side and 485 feet on the opposite side, an imposing structure of yellow brick and white Pompeian terra-cotta. Soaring out of the main splash of color was White's prized tower, reaching 320 feet above the sidewalk and giving the square the city's tallest building except for the Pulitzer Building.

To prove that this was no mere facade, the architect also went slightly wild on the inside. Pale red walls enfolded an auditorium 200 feet by 350 feet, the largest then in existence, with seats for 8,000 persons and floor space for several thousand more, all laid out beneath an 80-foot-high ceiling. On the north-

The architect: Stanford White, the leader of the artistic renaissance endowing New York with new buildings, statues and monuments. His Garden is lavish, a Moorish castle that opens in 1890 with colonnade, tower, roof garden and theater.

White's castle promptly becomes the center of social life in Manhattan. Reflecting this life, *Harper's Weekly* portrays the Columbian Ball of 1893 inside the Garden, as drawn by Victor Perard, and the night crowd tarrying in top hats in the colonnade outside, as drawn by W. T. Smedley.

It is a time and a place for extravagant touches, heroic statuary, military pomp and circumstance. *Frank Leslie's Illustrated Newspaper* catches the Square in centennial splendor, with insets showing the Washington Square arch at lower left and the President's stand at upper right.

west corner of the complex, White created a theater with 1,200 seats; on the southeast side, a concert hall with 1,500 seats; on the southwest, an expanse to hold the largest restaurant in New York; and along the western flank, overlooking Madison Avenue, a roof-garden cabaret.

The grand entrance off Madison Avenue, alongside a Roman colonnade, gleamed with lavender marble. The tower rose from a base that measured thirty-eight feet on each side. An elevator shaft and a circular staircase led to the pinnacle, where, in the glare of ten searchlights, stood the great copper goddess Diana the huntress.

This was no run-of-the-mill goddess. For one thing, she towered eighteen feet into the city skies. That seemed a little out of proportion to the rest of the tower, even to Stanford White and the sculptor, his old ally Augustus Saint-Gaudens. So they packed her off to Chicago, where the Columbian Exposition people had no such reservations, and replaced her three years later with a thirteen-foot Diana.

Even at thirteen feet, this new Diana proved to be an Olympian figure high above the marble portico and immense auditorium of the new Garden. She even revolved on ball bearings so that her bow and arrow always pointed into the wind. But she in turn created a storm of another sort because Saint-Gaudens had fashioned her in a dazzling state of undress, a matter that provoked the *Philadelphia Times* to deplore "the depraved artistic taste of New York."

It was ironic, but one city's depraved artistic taste can become another city's artistic prize. Half a century later, after a career on top of Stanford White's tower and many travels, Diana finally found a permanent home—at the top of a grand staircase in the Philadelphia Museum of Art.

With such baubles and battles to be accounted for, the ultimate cost of White's newest contribution to the city's social life came to something like $3 million. But on the evening of June 16, 1890, the curtain went up and the show went on, and nobody cut corners on anything.

A full house of 17,000 first-nighters crammed the Moorish castle, paying up to $50 apiece for the privilege, although none quibbled—including Mayor Hugh Grant, Gov. David B. Hill, Gen. William Tecumseh Sherman, and almost the full membership of the Horse Show Association.

They were escorted to their seats by ushers dressed in yellow uniforms with white satin scarves and red waistcoats with silver buttons, which were also the creations of Stanford White. Two ballet companies performed, Eduard Strauss of Vienna conducted a concert and the *New York Times* pronounced the evening's program "one of the most brilliant ever witnessed within an auditorium in this city."

The entire thing, the *Times* continued, was "one of the great institutions of the town, to be mentioned along with Central Park and the bridge of Brooklyn." And once the tower was completed a year later, the *Century* minced no words at all in declaring: "We do not understand how we lived so long even half-content without it."

Half-content wasn't half-bad, though, the Garden management soon discovered. After the grand opening, sellouts were few and far between. Adelina Patti packed the place with her recitals, and so did Richard Mansfield with his Shakespeare readings. The internal-combustion engine inspired innovations like the automobile show, and the introduction of a banked track ushered in six-day bicycle races.

But Frank K. Sturgis, the president of the Garden, stayed busy chiefly counting the deficits. It cost $20,000 a month to operate the complex, rentals rarely brought in more than $1,500 a night, and a $2 million mortgage hung over the scene as relentlessly as Diana with her bow and arrow.

For a time Sturgis tried invoking a sure thing, the lure of boxing exhibitions, to fill the house during the long gaps in the schedule. But the surest of the sure things, John L. Sullivan himself, was appearing less often in the ring and more often on the stage in those days. In fact, when the Garden needed him most, John L. was off in the hinterlands touring with a road company that had enough trouble of its own with a melodrama titled *Honest Hearts and Willing Hands*.

Reaching for a substitute attraction, the new Garden came up with a new draw: James J. Corbett of San Francisco, who tried nobly to pack the place on the night of January 16, 1892, by going three rounds with each of three opponents. He beat them all, and before the year was out he even beat the once immovable John L. and lifted his heavyweight title. But because prizefighting was then going through one of its periods as an illegal pastime, the Garden was denied even that momentous

It is also a time of some struggling to keep the Garden filled between extravaganzas, and much of the struggling is done by Frank K. Sturgis, its president. He tries everything from six-day bicycle racing to Adelina Patti.

event. Instead, it was staged in New Orleans, and Sullivan was dethroned by a knockout while back in New York the Garden staggered along.

There were many nights when society went through the marble doorway, but not enough nights when the masses went through. For instance, one of the perennial bookings was the National Horse Show Association of America, Limited, which was founded at Delmonico's restaurant in 1883 and which promptly became a regular tenant of the Garden, staging its show the week before the opening of the opera and ushering in the fall and winter seasons in the area's shops and hotels.

The emphasis was placed on useful horses rather than decorative ones, and on a typical evening the arena was cluttered with 350 entries that included trotters, hunters, policemen's mounts, fire-engine horses, and even a few jackasses. The action, too, tended to be utilitarian. Mounted cops would pursue a "runaway" horse, just as they did in the streets outside every day, and a prize would be awarded to the policeman who turned the trick in the fastest time on the clock. Or, simulating the daily action in the city's fire houses, harnesses would be suspended above stalls at one end of the arena, and fire companies would race one another to see how speedily they could harness their animals to their engines and chase an imaginary fire.

After Stanford White designed the new Garden, a certain change in tone crept into the horse show. For one thing, as many as 600 horses were now entered each year. For another, they were now quartered in the basement of the building rather than in stalls outside. And what's more, society women began to take an interest in the show. They even began to furnish their arena boxes with chairs and rugs and other comforts of home.

The VIPs at times included dignitaries from Washington like President Chester A. Arthur as well as dignitaries from England like Lillie Langtry, the actress, who touched off a fuss one night by leaning over the railing and planting a kiss on the brow of her hunter, Pauline.

Pauline had just won a blue ribbon, but the city's sanitation commission was nonetheless outraged—so outraged that it attempted to pass an ordinance making it illegal to kiss a horse at the show. The ordinance didn't pass, and the commission never fully explained whether it was trying to protect the animals or the people from the dangers of kissing in public.

The most enduring, and controversial, attraction of Stanford White's Garden is Diana the huntress, a 13-foot goddess sculpted by Augustus Saint-Gaudens and installed with drawn bow high above the city's streets.

But the National Horse Show survived and even saw times of splendor, when banks of flowers graced the arena, and champagne was served in the boxes, and horses slept between performances on linen sheets decorated with the family crest. In fact, down through the years, the show missed only half a dozen dates in its history as one of America's longest-running productions: in 1887, when a wall in the Garden collapsed; in 1889, when construction of the new arena was being delayed; and in the war years of 1914 and 1943–45, generations later.

At the other end of the scale of social values, some energy was pumped into the Garden by promotional whirling dervishes like Harry M. Pollok and Daniel P. McKetrick, a pair of onetime newspapermen from the sports department of the *World*. They were known as the Dresden China Kid and Dapper Dan, respectively, because they were dudes with a dandy manner. At least they were dandy enough to notice that although prizefighting was legalized in 1896, it was outlawed again in 1900, and they quickly proposed a substitute.

In one respect they represented a throwback to the drumbeating zeal of Barnum, and they beat their drums from an office in the new Flatiron Building at Twenty-third Street, down the block from the new Garden. Their first extravaganza featured foreign wrestlers, whom they imported and booked with flair, starting with Yussiff Mahmout the Turk, who appeared with a bushy mustache and bare feet, and George Hackenschmidt, billed as the Russian Lion, who later abandoned the ring for life as a philosopher.

But the Turk and the Russian Lion were merely the opening act. They were followed by people on roller skates and bicycles, including Daredevil Schreiber, who steered a bike down a slope from the top of the arena into a tank of water, and a succession of physical-culture performers. But in spite of all this activity inside the white Pompeian terra-cotta walls, the Garden was still swamped in silence as often as in noise.

"Those physical-culture shows got us into trouble," Dapper Dan McKetrick remembered. "Big guys in trunks swinging Indian clubs. Big dames in tights. The cops would take one look at the dames or maybe the tights and start blowing whistles. They'd run in everybody in sight."

By the turn of the century, life inside the Garden was just as tacky, just as grand, and just as varied as life outside the Garden.

Opposite:
Despite disputes over money, architecture or goddesses, one thing is constant: setting up the circus every spring beneath the big top.

In 1900 Theodore Roosevelt and William Jennings Bryan raised the level of oratory within the hippodrome. In 1905 the first wine-and-spirits show made its appearance. And in 1906 Marvin Hart boxed four rounds with Mike Schreck, both men being declared "members of this club" to bypass the ban on boxing, while the customers were elected "associate members" for a $2 initiation fee.

This was only one generation after the early Garden had been kept alive by things like "the First Annual Show of Horses, Ponies, Mules, and Donkeys" and by the magnetic presence of John L. Sullivan, when the Circus Maximus atmosphere was enlivened almost single-handed by heroes like Sullivan. That atmosphere had even gained some verve at times, as when "Gentleman Jim" Corbett, having dethroned the great John L. a decade later, rented the Garden and staged a boxing exhibition for the benefit of his legendary victim.

But no one supplied more verve to the "central palace of pleasure" than the man who had created it, Stanford White. He was there on many evenings for the horse show, when it was calculated that the "average" society matron was bedecked in gown, wrap, and jewels worth $13,000. He was there on many evenings playing host to celebrities like Mark Twain in his red-curtained box. He actually stayed there many nights in the apartment he had designed for himself in the tower. And he even died there, on the night of June 25, 1906, in the Roof Garden, where the elite came to meet, eat, and dance the hours away.

It was, in fact, the opening night of the Roof Garden's supper club and theater, with a dazzling production of *Mamzelle Champagne* on stage and an equally dazzling audience of social demons at the dining tables. No man was more dazzling than White, the architectural brain behind the Brooklyn and Metropolitan museums, Pennsylvania Station, the Washington Arch, and dozens of other public and private monuments. Nor was any man more dazzling for the ill-kept secrets of his personal life, which in White's case centered on an army of beauties led by Evelyn Nesbit, a twenty-two-year-old Florodora girl and Gibson girl, one of the ranking belles of New York, the storied "girl on the red velvet swing," *and* the wife of the millionaire Harry K. Thaw.

These were no ordinary "principals" in an ordinary triangle;

they were superstars of public life and the passion that went with it. Their notoriety was guaranteed by the fact that New York had roared through the Gay Nineties with an intensifying interest in after-hours types and places, and the after-hours types rarely disappointed their audience. The most obvious formula was that wealth attracted beauty, or vice versa, and so contretemps of all varieties were as inevitable as the shift in emphasis from the country to the city. And when the emphasis reached the city, it could most often be found in the bustling restaurants, theaters, and supper clubs.

There Diamond Jim Brady set the pace with his gargantuan appetite and gargantuan girth, frequently accompanied by the "Belle of Broadway," Lillian Russell, known to her many intimates simply as Nell. They were a weighty pair, famous for their marathon feasts at Rector's, which sometimes started with several dozen oysters, half a dozen boiled crabs, and a few ducks before they really got down to the serious eating. After dinner, Nell could be viewed onstage as the star of an operetta or musical; after *supper*, she could be viewed as the star of the café society swarming into the night spots. She was a fetching figure, and a corseted figure, and her fabled love life created as many rumors as her fabled bouts with knife and fork.

Miss Russell was a blond singer of sorts from Clinton, Iowa, who arrived in the big city as Nellie Leonard and made her debut as a devotee of the English ballad. Her repertoire and her name were styled for the Great White Way by the impresario Tony Pastor, who supplied the *nom de guerre* of Lillian Russell, after which Nellie supplied the legends. Later, the Wall Street millionaire James Lewisohn, who was not one of her four husbands, supplied the personal devotion that subtracted nothing from her career or her girth.

Brady was a railroad-equipment salesman who was more formally known as James Buchanan Brady until he began to run with world-class social sprinters like Oscar Hammerstein, John W. Gates (also known as Bet-a-Million Gates), Gentleman Jim Corbett, and our old friend Stanford White. They were unmatched at the art of making money and, occasionally, blowing money. In both cases, they often repaired to one of the private rooms set aside for heavyweight gamblers in Richard Canfield's casino on Forty-fourth Street off Fifth Avenue, two doors east of Delmonico's new restaurant.

In the after-hours life of the Gay Nineties, nobody carries more weight than James Buchanan Brady, "Diamond Jim."

Brady plays his role on a huge stage: Madison
Square, where the elite meet.

It was a sensationally appointed place with a construction cost reputed to be a million dollars and with an art collection that rivaled any in the land. Canfield himself was a tall, elegant person with a grammar school education, a record in prison as a felon, and a wide knowledge of art and literature, earned the hard way along with his fortune.

Like some of his chief clients, Canfield was a close friend of J. P. Morgan, with whom he shared a runaway interest in oil paintings. He also was an intimate of James McNeill Whistler, who once painted Canfield's portrait, which later was purchased by the Cincinnati Museum. He also made a mint of money on the stock market tips dropped by his distinguished customers at the gaming tables, and he probably expressed the ruling attitude of the day when he observed, "I do not know that I have any code of ethics. As morals are considered by most people, I have no more than a cat."

To the public, watching from the wings, this attitude could be applied more or less accurately to many of the *bon vivants* who moved in the same social circle. The notion was supported by the gossip that grew from their escapades in the night, especially when their stag parties reportedly broke the bounds of "accepted" behavior.

One legend sprang from a dinner party given by James L. Breese, a well-heeled bachelor, who placed a "Jack Horner pie" in the center of the main table. At the crucial moment, the pie was drawn open by ribbons and out stepped a gorgeous creature "covered only by the ceiling."

On another occasion, Stanford White served as the host at a birthday party for Diamond Jim and ten other guests in White's apartment in the Madison Square Garden tower. At dessert time, the waiters carried in a gigantic "Jack Horner pie" and placed it on the table in front of the guest of honor. Stanford White obligingly handed a ribbon attached to the pie to each of the diners, and when the assembled gentlemen yanked on their ribbons, out danced a young lady. To keep anybody from suffering acute melancholia, White also flung open the doors to the suite and in danced eleven other lovely young things to make the evening complete.

Lillian Russell and Evelyn Nesbit were not party girls of this sort, or even show girls in the narrow sense. They were queens of the cast, but they probably owed their opportunities to the

When Diamond Jim steps out, he is usually accompanied by Lillian Russell, the belle of Broadway. She sings, acts and even leads patriotic rallies in Union Square.

Behind the scenes: Mac Levy's gymnasium in the Garden packs them in, even for workouts. But then, the workouts sometimes feature uncommon fighters like Jack Johnson.

half-dozen chorus girls known as the Florodora Sextette, who filled the Casino Theater for 500 nights and forged a strong link between the money men out front and their devotion to the standard of beauty onstage. They wore pink walking costumes, huge black picture hats, long black gloves, and smiles, and they strolled onto the scene carrying parasols.

Watching them many evenings was Stanford White, who reserved an orchestra seat for every performance whether he attended or not. The girls did all right in life, too. One married a silk manufacturer, another a financier, another a diamond miner, another a Wall Street broker; one even took the vows with the nephew of Andrew Carnegie. The sixth, Marie Wilson, married Freddie Gebhard, formerly the suitor of Lillie Langtry and a society horseman whose jumper Leo had set an indoor record of six feet six inches at the National Horse Show in the Garden. Not only that, but Freddie's record-setting horse also added to the gossip by occupying stall space next door to Lillie's show horse, Pauline.

Anyway, all six of the original Florodora girls married millionaires, which provided America with a message in a time when nothing succeeded like success.

Evelyn Nesbit, a Florodora girl though not one of the "originals," did all right too. She not only maintained a relationship with Stanford White, but she married Harry Thaw, a thirty-five-year-old millionaire from Pittsburgh, whose hair-trigger temperament induced long periods of brooding about what might have happened in the days when his bride had been one of the notches in the architect's belt.

They were all there on the night of June 25, 1906, in the roof theater of White's Madison Square Garden, dining and drinking and brooding. Near the end of the second act, half a dozen girls in pink tights were dancing around an immense bottle of champagne while a tenor sang "I Could Love a Thousand Girls," and that may have been the last straw for the sulking husband.

Thaw rose from his table to leave the roof cabaret, and Evelyn dutifully rose and left with him. Then Thaw turned and walked back inside. He went straight to the table where Stanford White was sitting with his twenty-year-old son Lawrence and a group of friends, drew a pistol from beneath his black cloak, and fired three times in the direction of White's distinguished red head.

Diana commands the tower, where Stanford White lives and loves—and even dies, from a volley of bullets fired in the roof cabaret in 1906 by Harry Thaw, the enraged husband of Evelyn Nesbit, "the girl in the red velvet swing."

At the trial, Evelyn played her finest role. Dressed demurely in a pleated skirt and middy blouse with a large bow at her throat, she testified that she had met White in 1901, when she was barely sixteen. She said that the architect had drugged and seduced her in an apartment over the F. A. O. Schwarz toy store on Twenty-fourth Street. And later, she said, she had described this ordeal to Thaw just before their marriage.

As a result of her testimony, the trial caused a rise of 100,000 copies a day in the combined circulation of New York's newspapers. Also as a result of her testimony, the trial ended in a deadlocked jury. So in 1908 a second trial was called, and this time Harry Thaw was found not guilty by reason of insanity and was sent to the Matteawan Hospital for the Criminally Insane.

Irvin S. Cobb, later renowned as a folk humorist, covered the trial for the *World* and wrote that Evelyn Nesbit was "the most exquisitely lovely human being I ever looked at." The jury apparently agreed, especially after the prosecutor, William Travers Jerome, asked rhetorically, "Will no one say one word for Stanford White?"

No one did. After all, he had lived dangerously all his life and he had paid the penalty. Some, though, suggested that the penalty was a trifle harsh. They included Richard Harding Davis, the celebrated correspondent, who wrote such a moving defense that he, too, paid a penalty: His books were ordered removed from a library in New Jersey.

So Stanford White, who had lived and loved in his own Madison Square Garden, died there as well. And to the end, his greatest monuments were the goddesses he had installed there.

Prancing into the realm of the huntress, a
famous hunter: Buffalo Bill Cody.

5 JACK DEMPSEY'S MAN

Shooting Stanford White on the roof of his own shrine on Madison Square, while the tenor sang "I Could Love a Thousand Girls," was a tough act to follow. And for several years, while the world edged toward "the war to save democracy," the Garden didn't even come close.

In 1907, in the lull between the trials of Harry Thaw, the star performer in the arena was, in fact, a fox terrier named Champion Warren Remedy. He became the first dog to win the new best-in-show award of the Westminster Kennel Club, and he kept winning it for three straight years.

In 1908 the star performer was a frail little Italian with a handlebar mustache and an international reputation that he had just won at the Olympic Games in London. His name was Pietri Dorando, and he had created a sensation at the Olympics by finishing first in the marathon.

Well, he finished first, but he had help—and that's what created the sensation. After surviving the twenty-six miles from Windsor Castle to the White City Stadium, the classic distance for the marathon since the time of the ancient Greeks, the mustachioed little Italian lurched into the stadium all by himself. But those final 385 yards proved too much. He collapsed in the homestretch and was half carried and half dragged across the finish line by well-wishers and even officials in the huge crowd.

After that, Dorando was carried off to the hospital while people began to question the strange ending to the race. He was still in the hospital when a decision was reached. Since he hadn't actually completed the race, first place had to be awarded to the first man who did, Johnny Hayes of the United States. But in the deluge of grief and emotion that followed, Pietri Dorando had the last laugh. He received a gold trophy from Queen Alexandra, who had been touched by his ordeal, and he then trotted off to America as a professional to capitalize on his new status as a celebrity.

Trotting right on his heels came Johnny Hayes, and it didn't take much imagination to pair them as rivals in a return match. They were booked into the Garden before a sellout crowd that seemed to consist almost entirely of Italian Americans and Irish Americans, all of them chanting with passion. The trigger of the starter's gun was pulled by Richard Croker, the boss of Tammany Hall, and two hours and forty-four minutes later Dorando crossed the finish line about sixty yards in front of Hayes. This time nobody carted him home.

The two old Olympic rivals staged their match race just two years after the first national championships held by the Amateur Athletic Union in the Garden. But nothing that happened at the AAU meet—including five victories by Martin Sheridan of New York's Irish-American Athletic Club Whales—could equal the frenzy that they touched off in the marathon. They even generated a kind of national hysteria for the marathon. So much so, that an Irish runner named Matthew Maloney sat in the Garden brooding about his hero's defeat by Dorando, then went home for a short rest and finally did something to work off his exasperation. He ran fifteen miles north to Yonkers, got there in time to line up for a marathon that was just getting under way, and somehow lasted nineteen miles in the race before collapsing. And nobody carted him across the line, either.

In the same autumn of 1908, domestic politics joined international politics in the Garden. William Howard Taft campaigned for the presidency there, as Theodore Roosevelt and William Jennings Bryan had done before him, and as Woodrow Wilson, Teddy Roosevelt, Warren G. Harding, and other candidates would do after him. But the public response seemed a lot less spontaneous than it had seemed for the brief and violent contest between White and Thaw, or between Johnny Hayes and Pietri Dorando.

Nor was the excitement as great when Alfred Gwynne Vanderbilt succeeded Cornelius Fellowes as president of the National Horse Show, which was as old as the Garden itself. In

1909, when Vanderbilt took charge, the horse show needed some new pizzazz as badly as the Garden did. So he followed the formula that had helped make the marathon matches work—international competition. A team of British cavalry officers was invited to ride against a team from the United States, with cash prizes posted by the Hotel Association of New York.

The horsemen steered their mounts over four-foot stone walls, fences, and rails. And after Lt. I. S. Martin of the home team had won the match aboard a brown gelding named Connie, the event was reported in the *New York Commercial* as though it were a showdown in diplomacy:

> The invasion of the British officers has done much to make the Garden a lively place and the show a success. While tumultuous in their cheering, the onlookers were impartial and the pluck of the British officers in charging at the jumps brought out as hearty applause as any vouchsafed the Americans. There were cheers when the blue-ribbon was attached to Connie's bridle and the band played "The Star-Spangled Banner."

Within a year, teams from France and the Netherlands were riding and jumping their horses in the Garden. And within four years, women were riding astride for the first time. Not only that, but Mrs. Loula Long Combs even scored first in one class against men, and Mrs. John Gerken of Brooklyn became the first woman judge at the show. She said later that she had received several abusive letters for her trouble.

Teddy Roosevelt, who once had been described by Mark Hanna as "that damned cowboy," announced in 1912 that "I feel like a bull moose," and tried to stampede his way back into the White House in a three-cornered race of his own. He personally raised the rafters with his campaign speeches in the Garden, but by then the rafters and walls of the twenty-year-old "palace of pleasure" were growing a little drab. It was the old problem—keeping the place profitably filled often enough to pay the bills—and now the sparkle was even wearing off the facade of the great hall that Stanford White had designed a generation earlier.

In fact, two years after White's dramatic departure, the board of directors took a long look at the deteriorating arena and concluded that the walls were getting as dreary as the budget. These were the same men, or the successors to the same men, who had joined J. P. Morgan in pooling their resources eighteen years earlier—three million dollars, to be exact—for the construction cost of the yellow brick and terra-cotta building that had been heralded as "one of the great institutions of the town."

But the great institution had quickly become a great loser financially, even though it counted some great successes artistically. Perhaps the problem grew from the passing of the super-showmen like Barnum, who had died in 1891, not long after the new Garden opened for business. Perhaps it was the passing of the Victorian Age of stratified splendor and the turn into the twentieth century, a time when the horse and buggy were replaced by the motorcar, airplane, and long-distance train; a time when people began to have more choices than before. Perhaps it was just the passing of time and the inevitable change in the way of living and of earning a living, with factory life overtaking farm life and the "dismal science of economics" making its mark on everybody's life.

It was a change that William Jennings Bryan portrayed in one of his memorable speeches, in a lifetime of memorable speeches, when he bombarded the Gold Standard before the Democratic National Convention in 1896 in these soaring words:

> The man who is employed for wages is as much a businessman as his employer; the attorney in a country town is as much a businessman as the corporation counsel in a great metropolis; the merchant at the crossroads store is as much a businessman as the merchant of New York; the farmer who goes forth in the morning and toils all day, who begins in the spring and toils all summer, and who by the application of brain and muscle to the natural resources of the country creates wealth is as much a businessman as the man who goes upon the Board of Trade and bets upon the price of grain; the miners who go down a thousand feet into the earth or climb two thousand feet upon the cliffs and bring forth from their hiding places the precious metals to be poured into the channels of trade are as much businessmen as the few financial magnates who, in a back room, corner the money of the world.
>
> . . . Having behind us the producing masses of this nation and the world, supported by the commercial interests, the laboring interests, and the toilers everywhere, we will answer their demand for a Gold Standard by saying to them: you shall not press down upon the brow of labor this crown of thorns, you shall not crucify mankind upon a cross of gold.

Bryan won admiration and nomination, but lost the election. Even the Republicans conceded that he was a powerful man on the speaker's platform, and nobody quarreled with his general

Under the same roof that covers bicycle riders, fighters and wrestlers, the Garden Theatre offers a kind of culture oasis with its own stage, lobby, box office and stars. Yes, even Sarah Bernhardt.

They come to see the newfangled gadget of the new century, too: the radio, which takes over the place with its own "show."

They also come to see some other newfangled things: bathing beauties, for want of a better term, lined up in a contest in 1920.

observation that times were changing, even if you did not embrace his oratory or his precise picture of the new industrial society.

One thing was sure in Manhattan as the new century opened: The "magnates" of Madison Square Garden were finding it just as tricky as anybody else to round up the "producing masses." At least, to round up enough of the masses often enough to keep the house solvent. Whatever the cause, whatever the shift in emphasis that influenced people's pursuits and purses, times were growing hard. So the directors finally voted in 1908 to stop absorbing their losses, and they placed the entire operation on the market.

It took a while to find a taker, especially one with the asking price of $3,500,000. But three years later the asking price was whittled down, and a real estate concern known as the F. and D. Company bought the complex. It soon became clear, however, that a real estate company could not routinely succeed in running an entertainment showplace as a stepchild, or an investment. Five years later, with America drawing closer to the war already wracking Europe, the company called it quits and went bankrupt.

Holding the bag, so to speak, was the New York Life Insurance Company, because it was holding the mortgage for $2,300,000. So the insurance people foreclosed, and New York Life became the next owner of a "great institution" with a memorable past and a memorable debt.

It was, however, not the best of times for an insurance company to be running an entertainment showplace as a stepchild either. More and more people were getting caught up in the new austerity. And when they looked for some escape, they seemed to be heading outdoors. But even the outdoor arenas had to be financed without city, county, or federal support; and except for the involvement of a brewery or some other local business, it was not yet common for arenas to be financed with corporate support either. It was strictly a matter for personal plungers like Charles Ebbets, John T. Brush, Clark Griffith, and Connie Mack, all of whom built or rebuilt their own baseball stadiums.

Then World War I fastened its grip on things, and the business of entertainment temporarily became the wrong business at the wrong time.

As a result, New York Life found itself holding the bag again.

For a time the company considered transforming its investment into something more profitable, like an office building or some other property with a future. But every time the decision came near, public pressure surfaced—since the Garden had always been intertwined with the political life as well as the social life of New York—and the decision was postponed.

Each postponement, though, provided a new lease on life for Barnum's old Hippodrome center. And new life was finally breathed into the old lease with the arrival onto the scene of a roaring showman who would carry the place into the Roaring Twenties, a traveling promoter and onetime operator of saloons from Nevada to Alaska, George Lewis "Tex" Rickard.

But a new force is needed to rescue the Garden from its financial straits, and brawn replaces beauty. Tex Rickard's the name.

"Tex Rickard was in fact a gambler," Jack Dempsey remembered in his memoirs.

> When he won, he won big; and when he lost, he lost big. In his early days, he discovered he had a natural instinct for promoting —anything and everything. Once he had put a purse filled to the brim with twenty-dollar gold pieces in the window of his Northern Bar Saloon to sell tickets to a Joe Gans fight. Seeing gold displayed turned out to be quite a come-on. Within three days, the fight was completely sold out.
>
> Rickard, a solitary man since being orphaned at 10, grew up on a Texas ranch. He had been a cowhand, a wrangler and later a Texas sheriff. He had been in the Klondike gold rush and had struck it rich in the famous Bonanza strike. With the money, he set up a saloon and gambling hall, only to lose it all eventually on a bad wager. He lumberjacked for a spell and then returned to the action. Some time and money later, he opened another saloon and became even wealthier before losing it all again on worthless gold claims. His Northern Bar Saloon was just about his last venture in the West. From the time I met him, I treasured his friendship and loyalty.

It was probably natural for Jack Dempsey to find common cause with Rickard because he, too, had been a roamer out of the West. They were, in fact, like two answers looking for a question. And they found it together, in the East.

It was also natural because Rickard developed a passion for prizefighting, a passion that he turned into a profit as early as 1906 after he had risked $33,500 bidding for the promotional rights to the lightweight-title fight between Joe Gans and Battling Nelson. He won the rights and made money, and four years later he was back in business with another promotion: Jack Johnson against Jim Jeffries for the heavyweight title in Reno.

The fight had all the earmarks of Rickard's strange genius for arousing the public. Jeffries had won the title back in 1899 by knocking out Bob Fitzsimmons, who two years earlier had won

Rickard arrives with a reputation as a gambler and promoter. More important, he arrives with a hell-bent young fighter named Jack Dempsey, who arrives (right) with his manager, Jack Kearns, to sign for his heavyweight title fight against Jess Willard.

With Willard brutally beaten in 1919, Rickard moves into the Garden immediately with straw hat, vest, bow tie and the new champion, Jack Dempsey.

it by knocking out James J. Corbett, the conqueror of John L. Sullivan. After holding the title for four years, Jeffries let it lie idle for a couple of years and then retired in 1905. Five years later Rickard came along to tempt him out of retirement to try a comeback against the black hero, Jack Johnson.

The match was handled by Rickard and Jack Gleason of San Francisco, who offered the headline purse of $101,000, with 60 percent going to the winner and 40 percent to the loser, who turned out to be the thirty-five-year-old Jeffries by a knockout in the fifteenth round. Each man got $10,000 for training expenses, and each sold his picture rights for $50,000 or more. So the cash and the glamour were there. And to make sure that they stayed there, Rickard himself climbed into the ring and served as the referee.

Six years later, after a detour to Paraguay for a fling at cattle ranching, Rickard turned up in New York, where boxing now was legal if it complied with the Frawley Law: no knockdowns, no decisions. It was the era of "newspaper decisions," when the sportswriters at ringside rendered the verdict in print in a sort of throwback to the "exhibition" days when John L. Sullivan gave his boxing demonstrations in the old Garden. But whatever the rules, Rickard was impressed. He promptly borrowed $10,000 from a ticket broker named Mike Jacobs, leased the Garden from New York Life, and matched the new heavyweight champion, Jess Willard, against Frank Moran.

Willard got the decision from the newspapermen and also got $47,500, a record for an indoor fight. Tex Rickard got a gate of $152,000, the biggest in the Garden's history. The Garden got another lease on life, and before long it joined forces with the tough-talking saloonkeeper in an alliance that helped to revive the spirits and the bank account of the threadbare building on Madison Square.

The alliance was forced to wait for a couple of years because the war was steepening in Europe, but meanwhile the stage was being set for a decade of "release" that would bring tumultuous changes and a new public zest for all forms of entertainment. At least the future stars of the cast were taking their places in the wings. They included the directors of New York Life, who were biding their time with their white elephant; Tex Rickard, who was busy shaping the career of his newest discovery, Jack Dempsey; and the dapper little politician and social tiger James J. Walker, who later would symbolize the new era as the swinging mayor of a swinging city but who, for now, was pursuing a career that would make him Democratic leader of the New York State Senate and the redeemer of professional boxing.

Not only that, but the city itself was preparing for a revival of the arts, chiefly the manly arts. It was a time when the sporting world and the theater world were renewing the close ties that had enlivened Manhattan a generation earlier, and these ties already were evident in the well-worn circles traveled by people like John McGraw, the manager of the Giants and a crony of Rickard and Dempsey.

McGraw had been making waves in New York since he arrived from Baltimore in 1902 and started winning pennants and fistfights. He was a master of the rough-and-tumble and the natural enemy of almost anybody who cared to look his way without affection. His philosophy was simple: "The main idea is to win." Gene Fowler once described him succinctly in these words: "Stoutly knit, as game as a pit-bird, he was very much in earnest when socking time was declared." And Grantland Rice once observed, "His very walk across the field in a hostile town was a challenge to the multitude."

He also possessed a flair for attracting attention as well as brickbats, whether he was winning or losing. In 1916 his baseball team, the toast of the town for years, opened the season by losing eight straight games. Then McGraw began moving players around the field like chess pieces, and they suddenly won seventeen straight, and on the road at that. Then he traded the legendary Christy Mathewson to Cincinnati, noting that "he was not only the greatest pitcher I ever saw, but he is my friend, and he is ambitious to become a manager, so I have helped him to gratify that ambition."

Later the same summer, after another series of trades, the Giants unexpectedly pieced together the longest winning streak in baseball history. Starting on September 7, when they beat the Brooklyn Dodgers, they won twenty-six games in a row. And they still finished the month and the season in fourth place in an eight-team league.

The following spring, the Giants were barnstorming their way from their training camp in Texas to New York. On April 6 they read on the bulletin board of the local newspaper in Manhattan, Kansas, that President Wilson had asked Congress to declare war on Germany. But in the spirit of the times, McGraw stayed busy fighting his own wars. In June he took a swing at an umpire named Bill Byron, also known as "the singing umpire" because he had a habit of humming between pitches. He was fined $500 and suspended for sixteen days by the president of the National League, John K. Tener, whom he promptly denounced as a tool of the Philadelphia Phillies.

They finally survived all the battles and won the pennant, only to lose the World Series to the Chicago White Sox. Then,

December 14, 1920: the Roaring Twenties begin with a roar.
Dempsey defends his title in the Garden, and keeps it by knocking
out Bill Brennan in the twelfth round of a tough fight. Now the doors
are open to new prosperity and new commotion in the Garden, from
six-day bicycle races to Boy Scout jamborees . . .

. . . and beneath a tower sign proclaiming the opening of a swimming pool in 1921, Rickard converts his arena into a public playground. But his heart, and his money, belong to one thing, the thing that kept Garden II going: the prize ring.

as McGraw was leaving the field after the final defeat, he passed the manager of the Chicago team, "Pants" Rowland, who said, "Mr. McGraw, I'm sorry that you had to be the one to lose." McGraw glanced up and snarled, "Get away from me, you damned busher."

Jack Dempsey, later describing the maneuvers that brought him into this company of free-swingers and free-drinkers, remembered a conversation with his manager, Jack Kearns.

> He told me he'd hooked up with Tex Rickard, the guy who'd built the stadium for the Jack Johnson–Jim Jeffries fight, the one in which Johnson had pushed Jeffries through the ropes. And then the words poured out:
> "When I arrived in New York, I met a pal and we went to the Biltmore. There I spotted Wild Bill Lyons. You remember, he had been a sergeant-at-arms in the Colorado State Senate. He joined us along with John McGraw (I knew him in my Klondike days), and pretty soon we got to talking and drinking when that Rickard came along. You know, kid, when McGraw introduced us, that crafty, shiftless gambler pretended he'd never set eyes on me before. Gave me that crap: Say, haven't I seen you somewhere? Damn right he had, so I set him straight by telling him that I had been the gold weigher in his Northern Bar Saloon. He sure didn't like me reminding him, kid. But he played it straight and then said that maybe he did recognize me, but I had changed. We then got to talking about this and that, and I told him all about you, how I was your manager and all."

The drinking bout led to the crucial bout in Toledo, Ohio, on the Fourth of July in 1919, in which Dempsey wrested the heavyweight championship from the 260-pound Willard in three brutal rounds. The fight drew a lot of attention. The Ohio Ministerial Association denounced it, and the Ohio legislature voted a resolution asking the governor to ban it. But it also drew 19,650 customers, who paid a total of $452,224, and later the promoter—Tex Rickard, naturally—pocketed a profit of $85,732.

Now Rickard held the winning combination. He held a lock on Dempsey's future fights and he held the attention of Madison Square Garden. He also got the support of another member of the cast, Jimmy Walker, who steered a bill through the legislature in Albany that, once and for all, cleared prizefighting as a legal business.

It was 1920 when Walker's bill made it, the war in Europe

was past, and Rickard wasted no time in parlaying all the elements into a winning hand. He signed a ten-year lease with New York Life for $200,000 a year, painted and repaired the old Garden, and played a commanding role in spiraling it into the Era of Wonderful Nonsense.

6 TEMPLE OF FISTIANA

In 1920, while Johnny still came marching home from the trenches of Europe, the American public lunged hungrily into its "roaring" decade of heroes and hooch.

The New York Yankees bought Babe Ruth, who promptly repaid the debt by hitting fifty-four home runs. The Notre Dame football team, led by an all-America fullback named George Gipp, played nine times and won nine times. The colt Man O' War went to the races eleven times and won eleven times. A tennis prodigy named William Tilden became the first American to win the men's singles championship at Wimbledon. And Jack Dempsey defended his new heavyweight title by knocking out Bill Brennan in twelve rounds in Madison Square Garden.

It was a time of heavyweight performers in all sports, and the point was not lost on Tex Rickard, the new impresario of the Garden, who proved that he was an exceptionally fast man with a buck. Sixty days after the Walker Law legalized boxing in New York State, he signed his ten-year lease with the New York Life Insurance Company and became the ringmaster of the Garden. Thirty-four days after signing, he staged the first fight under the new law, with the lightweight Joe Welling taking the decision over Johnny Dundee. Ninety days later he had Dempsey in the ring with Brennan. And five years later he counted the total take from boxing in the Garden at $5 million.

This was a far, far cry from the days when the first ringmaster of the place, P. T. Barnum, had rented the Garden for $5,000 a year for his waltzing elephants and acrobats. It was also a far cry from the days when Stanford White had served as the resi-

June, 1924: From Diana's perch to the Square below, flags and bunting hang in spotlights for the Democratic National Convention, which turns into a marathon.

dent genius of the second Garden and had strung 6,600 of Edison's new lights around the walls on its opening night in 1890 while two huge searchlights bathed the eighteen-foot statue of Diana on top of the tower—but while the nightly rent of $1,500, meanwhile, fell short of the house's basic expenses, which started at $20,000 every month just to operate the place. And it was a far cry from the scrambling early days of the new century when Barnum and White were gone and Rickard had not yet arrived from the West.

In between the reigns of the impresarios, people had tried to keep the old arena filled with an endless variety of events, all of which lacked a theme and a winner.

In 1891, the year after the doors were opened to the new Garden on Madison Square, they installed the first six-day bicycle race on a sloping indoor track. In 1892 the first Winter Sports Show was held, along with the Poultry Show and the Flower Show. And Adelina Patti even sang "Home, Sweet Home" with the massed support of a chorus of 1,000.

A year later, the Shrine Carnival caused a sensation with its Nautch Girl Dance, the pioneer hoochie-coochie. Three years later, William Jennings Bryan, fresh from his "cross of gold" oration in Chicago, received formal notice of his nomination for president in the Garden and responded with a two-hour speech that slowly cleared the hall. Four years after that, undismayed, he returned for another campaign appearance and drew record crowds, but he lost again to William McKinley. The first Automobile Show, also in 1900, helped put America on wheels. The first Wine and Spirits Show, in 1905, drew appreciative crowds, though it lacked the impact of the Sportsman's Show, when 5,000 bees somehow got loose among the customers. None of these had the curiosity value of the first professional football game with college stars like Glenn "Pop" Warner and Buck O'Neill. And few of these events came close in terms of excitement to the first boxing championships of the Amateur Athletic Union in 1911, when Matt Wells beat Knockout Brown before a crowd of 10,000 that included "a lady" at ringside, who created more commotion than even Knockout Brown.

But the sum total of all such one-night stands (and even six-day races) was not quite equal to the sum of its parts because something was missing—a unifying force, a sure thing. In the old days, that sure thing had been a hero like John L. Sullivan,

who had stolen the thunder from London, long the capital of the boxing world, even when he was sparring with Joe Coburn, not long after Joe had been released from Sing Sing Prison. Those were the days when, the *New York Times* observed, "tier after tier of silver-headed walking sticks, opera hats, white shirt fronts and evening ulsters rose to the eaves, while a cloud of tobacco smoke ascended to the roof, obscuring the small boys who dangled their legs from the rafters."

They were the days, the *Times* reported, when the Garden "seemed a great people's hall or 'tabernacle,' where all, of whatever class, race, position or sect, were welcome, rich and poor, master and servant, side by side."

But eventually prizefighting was outlawed and the new Garden lost its sure thing. It also lost its sense of appreciation of the sure thing, and the profit that went with it. "There is," the *Times* later noted, casting a vote for better things, "no trace or flavor of the circus, the walking match or *pugilism* about this new Garden." How soon they forget.

But Tex Rickard did not forget. In fact, not for one minute did he forget that the decline of professional boxing in Madison Square Garden at the turn of the century had been accompanied by the decline of everything else. He also did not forget that the fight game thereupon had shifted to the West, where the frontier spirit still tolerated such things and where, in 1906, Rickard himself had taken his first plunge into promoting fights. And he certainly did not forget the result: 200 Pullman cars importing 7,500 customers with cash from around the country into Goldfield, Nevada, to pour $69,715 into the turnstiles to see Joe Gans beat Battling Nelson on a foul.

So, fortified by his memories, Rickard put two and two together and came up with four, and then some. He had absolutely no doubt that boxing was the right sport at the right time in the right place, and that the time was then, right after the war, and that the place was back east in the Garden. He had no doubt that prizefighting would regain the official blessing of New York State, either, not with Jimmy Walker steering the bill through the legislature as the Democratic leader of the Senate who also craved the chance for some ringside action of his own.

Most of all, he had the fighter—Dempsey, now the heavyweight champion and a hellcat performer. And if the Garden had drawn the fight mob through the gates once to watch Paddy

Slavin, Tom Sharkey, and Kid McPartland, to say nothing of wrestlers like Yussiff the Terrible Turk, Dr. Roller, Earl Caddock, Marin Plestina, Ernest Roeber, and William "the Great" Muldoon, later the chairman of the new state athletic commission—well, who could resist the animal attraction of "the Manassa Mauler"?

"That block-long Garden was by far the best," Dempsey recalled later, reconstructing the heady feeling.

> It was the center of sports life and entertainment in New York. In it appeared rodeos, balls, circuses such as the Buffalo Bill shows in which Annie Oakley shot glass balls out of the air, fights, exhibits and conventions.
>
> For the Brennan fight, I trained at the Van Kelton Tennis Courts on Fifty-seventh Street at Eighth Avenue. We were having trouble drawing crowds, so Teddy Hayes ran down the street to the Winter Garden and persuaded Al Jolson to come over and help

Tex Rickard, meanwhile, does some politicking of his own: he signs a young heavyweight named Gene Tunney while Tunney's manager, Billy Gibson, looks past the bottles that have found their way onto Rickard's desk.

me out. When the weather was nice, I worked out in Central Park, the same Central Park that had once provided me with a bench for the night.

Fourteen thousand people showed up for the fight. I was booed from the moment I stepped through the ropes. Not only was this going to be a tough fight with Brennan, it was going to be difficult with the fans, too. (I was still the favorite when it came to betting.)

Brennan had a vicious right as well as a long left, which really demolished me. One of my eyes swelled. An ear was torn. By the twelfth round, we were both beat, swinging at each other and missing. Then he caught me on my torn ear, but I didn't go down. I swung a left to his face and we fell into a clinch. When we came out of it, I put everything I had into a left to the stomach and a right hook to the heart. Down he went.

It was a time of passion, all right, from the speakeasies to the prize ring, where a man could hoot Dempsey because he had not served in the army and then could just as strenuously support him with a bookmaker. But Rickard could be all things to all people—gold-rush saloonkeeper to the riffraff, patron of the performing arts to the swells. As long as they had the inclination and the dollars, he provided the show. Sometimes he even provided a place for the public to play. Not long after the Dempsey-Brennan fight, he flooded the entire arena floor for an AAU swimming meet; then he used the site as a huge swimming pool for the customers. On other occasions, he built a wooden track around the arena for college footraces and then made sure the public would stay to the bitter end by announcing: "Dancing will follow the games." And, with the track cleared away, the floor became a gigantic ballroom.

Once he even went to the rescue of a damsel in distress, Anne Morgan, the daughter of the Garden's longtime financial angel, J. P. Morgan. She asked Rickard if she might borrow the arena for one night to raise money for her pet charity, the American Friends of France. This was not exactly Tex's cup of tea, but he handled it with grace and good manners and also supplied the main attraction of the evening—Benny Leonard, the lightweight champion, and Richie Mitchell, the pretender to the title.

"We signed for the fight right in the drawing room of the Morgan mansion on Madison Avenue," reported Francis Albertanti, the chief drum-beater for Rickard. "There were Leonard and Billy Gibson, his manager; Richie Mitchell and myself. Miss

Morgan smoked a cigarette in a long holder. There was a fire in the fireplace."

This was no floating barge in the Hudson River, safe from the prying eyes of the cops who might interrupt the signing ceremony; this was the drawing room of the Morgan mansion on Madison Avenue, with a fire in the fireplace. That's how far the fight mob had come so fast. But Miss Morgan paid a price of sorts for her role as a liberated woman. One critic said that she had "degraded womanhood" by taking part in such a rowdy enterprise, friend of France or not. Another suggested that she was "aiding the crime wave."

But she drew a black-tie audience to the Garden on a cold evening in January of 1921, and her audience dug down for $136,408 to join the adventure, with Leonard netting $40,000 and the American Friends of France $75,000. Rickard, with an air of benevolence, just smoked his cigar that night (without a long holder). Then, always in tune with the times, he capitalized on his new image by announcing that he would donate 10 percent of the take from each fight night to Mrs. William Randolph Hearst's Free Milk Fund, thereby assuring his good standing in the milk of human kindness with at least one especially strong side of the nation's press.

By now business was booming with fights, horse shows, track meets, and the circus. And for fifty cents a man down on his luck could buy a "home" for nearly a week in the balcony while the six-day bicycle races kept spinning around the boards below. In 1923 they brought in the Annual New York Roundup: Rodeo and Stampede, right in the middle of Manhattan. And in 1924 Hollywood made its debut by using the Garden as the background for the film *The Great White Way* with Anita Stewart. Later, Hollywood returned for *Madison Square Garden* in 1932 with Jack Oakie, William Boyd, and Zasu Pitts; and for *The Manchurian Candidate* in 1963 with Frank Sinatra and Laurence Harvey.

But for Rickard, there was probably no greater extravaganza in "the house that Tex built" than the Democratic National Convention of 1924, a stemwinder that kept the stage for sixteen days and 103 ballots.

In the earlier days, when the Republicans had their headquarters at the Fifth Avenue Hotel and the Democrats met next door at the Hoffman House, the politicians preferred to hold their rallies at Cooper Union. Their reasoning was simple and unassailable: Cooper Union was smaller and therefore easier to fill. You didn't run the risk of all those empty seats. But by the 1920s, every major-party candidate for president had staged a blockbuster in the Garden at least once, and often to wind up a campaign in the biggest and noisiest arena possible. And William Randolph Hearst, who owned a home and a newspaper, the *Journal*, within shouting distance of Madison Square, regularly rented the place through the years to whip up enthusiasm for his perennial campaigns for mayor, governor, senator, and even president.

No national convention had occupied the "new" Garden until the Democrats arrived in 1924, thanks in part to another benevolent gesture by Rickard: no rent. When the delegates swarmed in, they were greeted by a new blue-and-white paint job, by 3,500 flags hanging from the rafters, by armies of telegraph and radio technicians working out of the cleaned-up animal stalls, by stifling heat, and by pickpockets who had escaped a police dragnet designed specifically to get them off the streets. They were off the streets, all right. The convention opened on Tuesday, July 24, and by the fifth day William Jennings Bryan's pocket watch had been lifted, inside the arena.

The chief contenders for the title in the convention were William Gibbs McAdoo, the Georgia lawyer and former secretary of the treasury, who was also the son-in-law of Woodrow Wilson, and Alfred E. Smith, the New York lawyer who was then governor. Everybody else with a claim was hoping for a deadlock, and that's what they got.

For two tumultuous weeks the convention kept grinding toward its deadlock, while the Alabama delegation cast "twenty-four votes for Oscar Underwood" inside the hall and working girls leaned from their office windows to catch the noise outside the hall. At the height of the stalemate, Bryan—the golden voice of the party, but an aged golden voice now—gave another of his two-hour orations. But the delegates responded with a booing uproar that was joined by many of the 13,000 spectators in what was described as "the wildest scene that the Garden has witnessed, in the memory of those that took part in it." Elmer Davis reported in the *Times* that the incident had produced "more pugnacity, ill-feeling, bad blood and un-Christian ferocity than is seen in the Garden in a whole boxing season."

But the Democrats hold the stage and hold the public's attention while ballot after ballot is cast to break a historic stalemate. One week after the convention opens, umbrellas sprout in Madison Square as loudspeakers relay the proceedings from the arena to the rainy streets outside.

Opposite:
The main contestants are Alfred E. Smith and William Gibbs McAdoo. But after 103 ballots, the winner is John W. Davis. Then the weary Democrats go home and leave the Garden (lower right) to other political groups like the Progressive Party, which throngs the hall but completes its business in a lot less time.

Seated at an oval microphone in the center of the disturbance was a young concert baritone from the Northwest named Graham McNamee. He had arrived in New York three years earlier seeking fame and fortune, and he found it.

After his debut at Aeolian Hall, the critic of the *New York Sun* commented, "He sang with a justness, a care and style." Later, by the time McNamee was singing 150 times in one recital season, he evoked notices like this one from the *Times:* "Anyone who sings the air 'O Ruddier Than the Cherry' from Handel's 'Acis and Galatea' with such admirably flexible command over the 'divisions,' with such finished phrasing and such excellent enunciation as McNamee showed, is doing a difficult thing very well indeed."

He was still doing a difficult thing very well indeed after he had drifted into radio as a jack-of-all-trades and sports announcer for station WEAF, New York, one of the pioneers of the new industry. Without coaching or customs to guide him, McNamee broadcast the middleweight championship fight between Harry Greb and Johnny Wilson in September of 1923, then took on the World Series between the Yankees and the Giants a month later. He did it all with a cultivated delivery and a runaway sense of adventure, to wit:

> Then came the thrill of all time, all World Series and all sports. Babe Ruth stepped up to bat. One hit would mean victory for the Yanks, and for them the Series. It was another "Casey at the Bat," and the stands rocked with terrific excitement. John McGraw took the biggest chance of his historic life. He ordered Rosy Ryan to pitch to Ruth. The crowd faded into a blurred background. Cheering became silence. Ruth lashed out at the first ball. Ruth hurled his bat and his weight against the second. Ruth spun at the third. Ruth shuffled back to the dugout, head hung low. A picture of dejection.

So Graham McNamee was already a celebrity among celebrities at history-making events when the 1924 political season interrupted the 1924 baseball season. But his "finished phrasing and excellent enunciation" were in great shape as he made some history himself that summer. At Cleveland in June, he broadcast the Republican National Convention *alone.* And at the Garden in July, he clung to his microphone while Alabama clung to Oscar Underwood and the Democratic convention clung to its deadlock.

It became the longest tie in political history and in Garden

history, and McNamee was still there describing it when the Democrats finally compromised and nominated John W. Davis, the lawyer from West Virginia and former ambassador to Great Britain. And after all that, Davis was solidly beaten four months later by Calvin Coolidge.

Nobody knew it then, but the Democratic marathon came close to being the last hurrah for the "central palace of pleasure" that Stanford White had designed with its turrets, towers, and terra-cotta walls. Later that year, the New York Life Insurance Company announced that it would demolish the Garden and erect a forty-story headquarters for its main office on the site. But again Rickard had sensed the situation and was already passing the hat for an even grander creation of his own.

He passed the hat among a group of Wall Street financiers and businessmen whom he called, with understandable feeling, "my 600 millionaires." No desperation, no panic at the loss of his leasehold; he would simply graduate from tenant to landlord. Besides, the old Garden had not been built for prizefighting, and he had no trouble conjuring up a vision whose chief feature was an arena built specifically for boxing and other indoor sports. He also had no trouble conjuring up the money. His millionaires kicked in nearly $6 million to support his vision, and Rickard prepared to move uptown.

Twenty-five blocks uptown, to be exact, and several long blocks west. His choice for a location was the old trolley barn on Eighth Avenue between Forty-ninth and Fiftieth streets. Then he cast his eye on additional space in the direction of Ninth Avenue. His goal was to acquire 75,000 square feet on which to erect the building, and his goal was backed by people like John Ringling, Richard F. Hoyt, Walter P. Chrysler, Kermit Roosevelt, and other well-bankrolled types. He quickly dispelled any notion that his sense of history might not be as sharp as his sense of values: He could scarcely imagine, he said, giving it any other name than Madison Square Garden, regardless of the new geography.

Meanwhile, down on Madison Square, the show went on. The 1924 Olympics in Paris had produced a star of world quality, Paavo Johannes Nurmi, "the Flying Finn," and Rickard promptly brought him to town with his twenty-two world records.

The third Madison Square Garden gives way to the fourth.

Above, Emile Griffith enters the ring under a banner announcing the new Madison Square Garden Center, which Bob Hope helps open officially on Sunday, February 11, 1968.

Montreal Canadiens coach Toe
Blake watches the action from
behind his bench, and twenty
years later Rangers goalie
John Davidson guards the net.

Bob Cousy (14) in action against
the Syracuse Nationals and, below,
Willis Reed writhes in pain
during the fifth game of the
1969-70 NBA playoffs, in which
the Knicks won their first
championship.

Action in a Westminster Kennel
Club Show and a National Horse
Show.

Dolly Parton (left) and Janis Joplin...

...Mick Jagger (left) and Rod Stewart.

Frank Sinatra

Bing Crosby and Bob Hope
as they inaugurate the
present Madison Square
Garden, and candidates
Jimmy Carter and Walter
Mondale at the
Democratic National Con-
vention in July 1976.

The Roller Derby whirls,
and the best women sprinters in
the world approach the finish
line.

Olga Korbut captivates the Garden
crowd; Billie Jean King keeps a rally
alive.

A pair of dazzling skaters: Peggy Fleming (left) and Dorothy Hamill.

George Foreman goes to a neutral corner and, below, high jumper Franklin Jacobs sets a new world record at the Millrose Games in 1978.

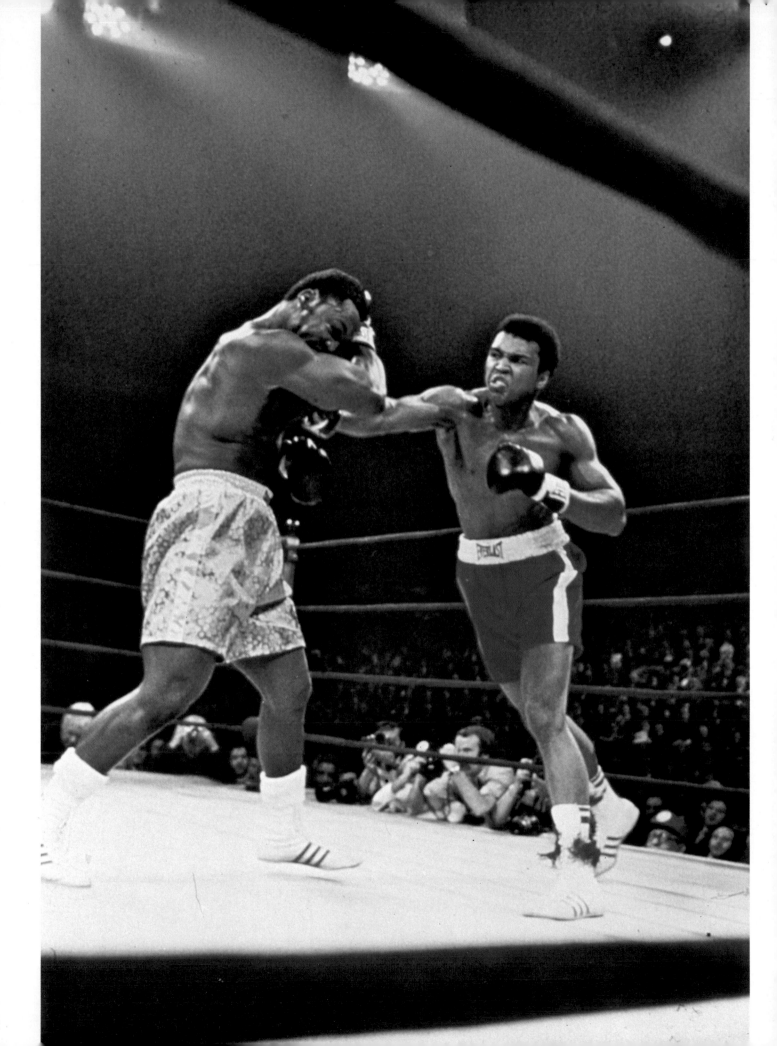

"The Fight of the Century":
At left, Muhammad Ali is on the
offensive, but here he is
about to hit the canvas for
the first time in his career.
Among those at ringside: Frank Sinatra.

Animal trainer Gunther Gebel-
Williams and the great clown Otto
Griebling.

Rickard already had scored a couple of coups in the importing business. In 1921 he brought Georges Carpentier from France to fight Dempsey on Boyle's Thirty Acres in Jersey City, and the buildup proved tremendous. At one point Tex disclosed that he had received formal "assurances" that Carpentier would head for America aboard the S.S. *Savote*. Then, while the ship sailed the Atlantic and the tension gathered, he inspired reports that the idol of all France was actually en route "with dozens of sportsmen from England and the Continent intent on witnessing the battle, in which Carpentier will attempt to wrest the world's heavyweight championship from Dempsey."

Georges didn't wrest anything from anybody. But after winning by a knockout in the fourth round, Dempsey could not help marveling at the whole show: "Tex was pleased, as I could see from the way he was puffing his cigar and tapping his cane. He not only had pulled the whole thing off successfully, but had also made history with a championship fight that lasted just about ten minutes."

Two years later Rickard reached into Argentina and extracted Luis Angel Firpo, "the Wild Bull of the Pampas," and that time the fight lasted only three minutes and fifty-seven seconds. But they were memorably violent minutes, during which Dempsey knocked Firpo down seven times in the first round alone and Firpo responded by knocking Dempsey clear through the ropes. Then Jack revived and threw the haymaker, and nobody asked for his money back after that one either. The fight was held at the Polo Grounds for the same reason the Carpentier fight had been held on Boyle's Thirty Acres: more seats were available outdoors than indoors.

But after Paavo Nurmi made history at the Olympic Games in Paris in the summer of 1924, Rickard aimed this newest international hero straight for the Garden. By the time Nurmi arrived that winter, he was already a legend. This is what he had accomplished in one week at the Olympics: On July 6 he ran the fastest 10,000 meters on record—in a training session. On July 8 and 9 he dominated the trial heats for the 1,500 and the 5,000 meters. With only an hour's rest, stopwatch in hand as always, he next won the 5,000-meter final. Two days later he led the Finnish team to victory at 3,000 meters in the preliminary heat. One day later, while twenty-four of the thirty-nine runners were quitting because of the torrid sun, he easily won at 10,000 me-

The Democrats are not the only distance runners in the Garden. Paavo Nurmi, the Finnish Olympic champion (right), arrives with Hugo Quist and heads for the boards.

ters. And the following day, he again led the Finns home first in the 3,000-meter final.

So he owned five new gold medals when he began barnstorming through the United States that winter, winning sixty-eight races, losing only one, and breaking thirty records. And on the night of January 6, 1925, he drew so many people to the Garden for the Finnish-American AC Games that the fire department finally ordered the doors closed.

Nurmi didn't disappoint anyone, either. He ran the mile against Lloyd Hahn and Joie Ray, the little cabdriver from Chicago, a five-foot-five-inch powerhouse who already had broken the world record for the mile during nine years of distance racing. But Joie met his match when the Flying Finn set a world mark for the mile in 4:13.6, covering the first 1,500 meters in 3:56 flat for another record; and ninety minutes later he outran his countryman Willie Ritola for another world record.

Three weeks after that, Nurmi defeated Ray in the Millrose

meet with world records at three-quarters of a mile (twice) and at a mile and a half (once). And still later, at the New York AC Games, he beat the field at two miles in 8:58.2, which was considered unthinkable, partly because it was 11 seconds faster than even the world outdoor record.

Three days after Nurmi's debut in the old Garden, the wrecking crews appeared uptown on Eighth Avenue and began to dismantle the trolley-car barns to make way for Rickard's new Garden. Then, four months later, the wreckers turned their muscle onto Madison Square to knock down the showplace that Stanford White had created there thirty-five years earlier. Even White's son joined the delegation of dignitaries who gathered on top of the tower to remove the architect's first goddess, Diana the huntress. Enclosed in burlap, she was carted away in a five-ton truck to a warehouse in Brooklyn. Fifty-six requests for permanent possession of the great copper statue were made to New York Life, which in the end granted her to New York University. But for twenty years Diana remained in the warehouse, with

After breaking thirty records during his American tour in 1924, Nurmi returns fifteen years later with Taisto Maki and receives the mayoral embrace from Fiorello LaGuardia.

bow drawn and arrow ready but without ever finding a niche on the campus, until she finally came to rest on top of the Great Stair Hall in the Philadelphia Museum of Art.

With the goddess gone for good, there was probably nothing left to do with the old "palace of pleasure" except to ring down the curtain and close the doors on the memories. They did that on the night of May 5, 1925, and the closing act, predictably enough, was a prizefight.

It featured Sid Terris, the lightweight, and Johnny Dundee, the favorite of the East Side, who had lost to Joe Welling in the first "legal" fight in the Garden five years before. Dundee lost this fight too, but the decision was overwhelmed by the weight of the evening's mood, which grew mournful. The arena was thronged with 10,106 persons, including Jimmy Walker, now the mayor; John Ringling North, the circus heir to Barnum;

Gentleman Jim Corbett, who enlivened the Garden during the eighteen-nineties as the conqueror of John L. Sullivan, surfaces a generation later and smiles on one of his successors, Jack Dempsey.

132

The Westminster Kennel Club show traces its history to 1877, which was two years before the first Garden opened. Now, in 1925, as the second Garden closes, it is still going strong.

William "the Great" Muldoon, the onetime wrestler now reigning as chief of the state athletic board; public figures like Jay Gould, Oliver Harriman, and Kermit and Teddy Roosevelt, Jr.; Tim Mara, the "legal bookmaker" who put the New York Giants on the professional football map; writers and artists like Damon Runyon, Grantland Rice, and Rube Goldberg; and fighting men like Kid McPartland and Jack Dempsey.

High above the ringside celebrities in the gallery, Rickard observed, sat many "very old men who looked as if they had been of some importance in days gone by."

Wherever they sat, they were there for the same reason, and it didn't have much to do with a twelve-round fight. They were there to witness the passing of an era. So was Joe Humphreys, the ring announcer, who had started introducing fighters on river barges in the days when the cops on shore stood ready to pounce on anybody involved in the "outlaw" sport. Joe was still doing his number now, generations later, calling for quiet in an authoritative voice with a richly exaggerated style that endowed any event with soaring significance. And this event did not escape his rhetoric.

"I wish to say," he announced from the center of the ring, in measured phrases, "that this marks the passing of this old arena that has stood the acid test these many years. Tonight we leave it for the last time. We mourn our loss, and take with us *fragrant* memories. . . ."

A voice from the balcony, picking up on that particular slip of the vocabulary, called down, "I can still smell them hot dogs and elephants, Joe."

Without missing a beat, Joe replied, still speaking in his best public-address manner, "The more I hear from guys like you, the more I believe in birth control."

Then, recapturing his funeral cadence, he continued:

"These memories will live forever in our hearts and in our minds. The great sport that made it stand out was boxing, and I want to pay tribute now to Tex Rickard and others I met within these portals."

A sergeant from New York's Sixty-ninth Regiment stood, pulled out a bugle, and played "Taps." Then Joe Humphreys led everybody in a chorus of "Auld Lang Syne," and finally reached the emotional peak of his evening by intoning a poem he had composed for the occasion. It ended with the lines

Farewell to thee, O Temple of Fistiana,
Farewell to thee, O sweet Miss Diana.

At ringside, a young politician named James A. Farley looked around as the crowd rose to leave, and said, "I hate to see it go down. But that's progress."

Then the mourners filed out through the smoke and the echoes of Joe Humphreys's elegy and, as they moved slowly up the aisles, Tex Rickard stood watching them. And holding his cane in his hand and marveling at what he had wrought, the onetime proprietor and resident genius of the Northern Bar Saloon shook his head and confessed:

"I never seed anything like it before."

They finally ring down the curtain on Garden II after 35 years, closing Stanford White's castle and Tex Rickard's "Temple of Fistiana" on May 5, 1925. But seven months later, Garden III opens farther uptown with a nonstop series of events. In one of them, Paul Berlenbach defends his light-heavyweight title against Jack Delaney.

7 GARDEN III
The House That Tex Built

It was a box of a building that extended 200 feet along Eighth Avenue and 375 feet down Forty-ninth and Fiftieth streets toward the Hudson River, only one block west of the Great White Way. It had triple tiers of seats connected by escalators, and it could handle 14,290 persons for the rodeo, 18,500 for the fights, and 5 million for everything on the agenda in a year's time. It had 10 microphones, 10 public-address speakers, and 29 spotlights and 296 other lights strung 79 feet above the arena. But it was still not exactly what Tex Rickard had in mind.

What he really envisioned, what he truly cherished as his dream house, was a roof over the Polo Grounds with the sides walled up for one chief purpose—to stage boxing matches by winter as well as by summer. But his associates, men of means and manners, dismissed his vision as fantastic, to say nothing of foolish.

Armed with a twenty-year contract as president of the new Garden at $30,000 a year, though, Rickard did not surrender entirely on either vision or principle. He also was armed with the memory that boxing and the circus had supplied the main events of Garden I and of Garden II, and he saw no reason to break up a winning combination. To clinch the point, he went on record with this valedictory as the demolition crews swarmed over the old Moorish castle where Barnum and Stanford White had painted the town red:

"I am sorry to say good-bye to the old place. It has been good to me, and I have had a lot of fun in it. I am also rather proud of the fact that I am the only man who made it pay."

The goddess of Madison Square is removed from her pedestal in 1925 and begins a new odyssey. The witnesses to history include, at the far left, Tex Rickard and Lawrence White, the son of the man who designed the splendors of Garden II.

He was bent on making the new place pay too. And with Thomas W. Lamb as the architect and James Stewart & Company as the contractor, it took only 249 days to create the house on Eighth Avenue where the elephants and heavyweights would show their muscles for the next 43 years. The theme was sounded on a plaque imbedded in the wall on the Fiftieth Street side that would have done justice to the Victorian rhetoric of Joe Humphreys:

"Dedicated to Athletics, Amusements and the Industrial Arts."

But the manly arts were not to be overpowered by the industrial arts. Even before the old Garden and tower were removed from the city's landscape, the New York Life Insurance Company received a letter on stationery headed "Benny Leonard, Lightweight Champion of the World," which read:

> It was with no small amount of trepidation that I read that the New York Life Insurance Company was contemplating tearing down Madison Square Garden. My interest in the old structure is purely sentimental, my thoughts being solely with the statue of Diana poised atop the tower.
>
> Diana has always been my goddess of luck. At every fight of mine at the Garden, I have made it a point to get a look at her before going into the ring. When the going was not so good for me, I thought of her while resting in my corner and always managed to rally.
>
> Now that you intend to raze the Garden and put in its place a modern office building, I feel moved to ask what is to become of the statue. Is it going to fall with the building; to be hauled away with the bricks, timbers and girders? Surely so lowly an end is not to come to her who has so gracefully hunted over the roofs of the city.
>
> Aside from my interest in Diana as my goddess of luck, I have great admiration for the statue as a work of art. Desiring to save it, I am requesting that you consider this letter a bid for the statue in case you should definitely decide to raze the Garden. I would make every effort to place it where everyone would appreciate its beauty and at the same time preserve my luck.

As things turned out, nobody was too moved by the thought of Benny resting in his corner during a tough fight invoking his goddess of luck. But even while Diana's future was being disputed and finally decided, Rickard made certain that Benny Leonard and his other gladiators would never go without a shrine of their own. In fact, in the early hours of the new Garden,

a preliminary fighter named George Godfrey arrived at his weighing-in ceremony forty-five minutes late. He had gone to the old Garden on Madison Square by mistake, and was forced to reverse course uptown in order to make his debut at the new "shrine" that Rickard was thoughtfully providing.

He also was thoughtfully providing two and a half rousing weeks of hoopla before the formal opening on the night of December 15, 1925. His chief allies were John Ringling, the circus man, and William Carey, the railroad man, and together they staged an "opening night" that lasted six full nights, starting on Saturday, November 28, with the six-day bicycle races.

They also made sure that nobody would overlook the inauguration or underestimate its significance as a civic event. Jim Farley, the Democratic party wheelhorse as well as a state boxing commissioner, fired the gun that launched the first race and the third Garden. And, because it was illegal to hold a profes-

Tex literally helps to build "the house that Tex built." It is situated at Fiftieth Street and Eighth Avenue, and it is dedicated to "athletics, amusements and the industrial arts."

sional sports event on Sunday, the stars of the second night's performance were the policemen who duly arrested a manager, a bike rider, and a pair of ticket takers. They called it an Arrest of Accommodation, and everybody was accommodated by a judge who fined the four official offenders $1 apiece before returning them to the scene of the crime, which by then was bustling with bicycle races. Not only that, but the ritual was repeated every year with good humor and good publicity.

For the record, the first winner of anything except judicial leniency was William Heinsberg, who won the initial bicycle sprint in the new Garden. The first title was won by Gerard Debaets and Alphonse Goosens, who had the highest team score at the end of the sixth consecutive evening of whirling. Then on December 6, to keep the place from going dark, they staged a basketball game as the next preliminary event, with the Original Celtics scoring 35 points and George Marshall's Washington Palace Five scoring 31. The gate totaled only $1,500, which confirmed Rickard's judgment that boxing paid the bills. But Tex quickly followed that bit of pioneering with a couple of sure things: Johnny Erickson upset the flyweight champion, Jack McDermott, and then on December 11, before a crowd of 17,675, Paul Berlenbach outpointed Jack Delaney to retain his world's light-heavyweight title.

Finally, after two and a half weeks of extravagant curtain raisers, the curtain was raised for good with an absolute novelty, a professional ice-hockey game staged with international flourishes before a sellout audience of 17,442. The teams were the New York Americans, who had been imported and virtually created for the occasion, and the Montreal Canadiens, who symbolized all the commercial and artistic pulling power of the National Hockey League.

The game was a novelty because ice hockey in 1925 was considered a "Canadian game" with no roots in New York's past and with no place in Rickard's future. But things changed after that rousing premiere. It was staged by Col. John S. Hammond, a former West Pointer who had captured Rickard's fancy in Argentina, where the colonel was serving as a military attaché and where the promoter was raising cattle in one of his many adventures. And now, back home front and center, Hammond introduced one of his pet productions to Rickard and the rest of New York.

He did it with plenty of flourishes, too. The West Point band not only showed up but also marched along Fifth Avenue to let people know something was up. From Ottawa, lending the international touch, came the governor-general's Royal Foot Guards band. From City Hall came the mayor, John F. Hylan, and from the wings came the mayor-elect, Jimmy Walker. All of them converged on the rink as the Garden presented its first "official" show.

The rink itself was royally jammed with colorful people before the skaters got down to work. Both bands paraded onto the ice in screaming uniforms, the governor-general's men in red coats topped by shakos and followed by the Montreal team in fiery red jerseys, then the West Point ensemble in dress uniforms and capes followed by the New York team in red, white, and blue studded with white stars.

Jimmy Walker, who rarely took a back seat to anyone, decided this time to play it straight and stood on the side while Mayor Hylan stepped out to the ice and "threw out" the first professional puck in the Garden's history. Eight minutes and five seconds later, Shorty Green—known to his mother as Wilfred—broke into the Montreal zone on the right wing, beat

Along with the new house comes a new tenant, the Rangers, who bring major-league hockey to the Garden. The Chicago Black Hawks supply the opposition in an early game in November 1926.

The heroes of the original Rangers include Frank Boucher, the gentleman on ice. He is so well mannered that he wins the Lady Byng Award for sportsmanship seven times and is fined for fighting only once. The skirmish costs him $15.

Billy Boucher to the puck, bore down on Herb Rheaume in front of the net, and drove home the first goal ever scored in Tex's house. But in the second period, Battleship Leduc—known to *his* mother as Albert—rammed one in for the Canadiens. Then Boucher put the visitors ahead and, in the final period, Howie Morenz put them safely ahead with the clincher. Final score: 3–1, Montreal.

No tears were shed, though, because Hammond and Rickard kept the act moving. Between periods they entertained the crowd with an exhibition of "fancy skating" by Gladys Lamb and Norval Baptie. And after the game they presented the Prince of Wales Trophy to the winners, an award that in later years went to the winners of the Eastern Division title in the league. Still later, Rickard made another of his fast calculations and decided that hockey teams, supported by hard-core customers, tended to make money. In this case, the money from the opening game was donated to the Neurological Institute of New York. But after that, Rickard decided, he would create his own team—not just a tenant team like the Americans—and donate the money to Madison Square Garden.

First he needed a franchise in the National Hockey League, but that proved no problem because the league had recently expanded south of the Canadian border into Boston with roaring success. So now an American division seemed inevitable, and another team in New York seemed inescapable. Second, he needed a nickname, and that proved no problem either: Tex's Rangers.

Finally, he needed someone to organize the club. And half a century later, this is how that step was remembered by George W. Goman, an amateur hockey player and winter-sports militant who had stopped by the old Garden in the summer of 1925 to ask about buying season tickets for the first year of the new Garden and who had left an hour later with something even better, a job as a hockey staff man:

> Colonel Hammond had been most impressed with Conn Smythe, who appeared at the Garden as coach of the Toronto University varsity with a squad of only nine players and easily defeated Yale and Princeton. Mike Jacobs, the unofficial power behind Ringling and Rickard, liked Smythe, too, and he was called down and hired.

As general manager, Smythe promptly signed his first Ranger

players, Murray Murdoch and Ching Johnson, a pair of memorable defensemen. Next he recruited Taffy Abel and the three men who formed the team's first line: the Cook brothers, Bill and Bun, and Frank Boucher. He did not exactly recruit Boucher, who had already been signed by Boston; he arranged to buy the center for $10,000. Consequently, Smythe was a trifle annoyed the next day when he began to announce his coup to Colonel Hammond, who interrupted him to say, "I just talked to the Bruins, and they're letting me have Boucher for $12,500."

It took only a few irritations like that one to inflame things between Hammond and Smythe, with the predictable result: Before the Rangers ever took the ice that fall, Smythe was the ex-general manager and his place had been taken by Lester Patrick, a solid citizen of hockey with wavy gray hair and the nickname "the Silver Fox." He and his brother Frank had just spent several years on the West Coast organizing and running the Pacific Coast Hockey Association, and George Goman remembered that transaction too:

> Lester had told friends he wished he was back in big-time hockey. We pressured Colonel Hammond and he finally let me put in a phone call to Lester in Victoria. I reached him and asked if he'd be interested in coming to New York for talks at the Garden's expense. He agreed, and left the very next day by train. It was a long trip and I met him at Grand Central and took him to the Biltmore, then to dinner, and gave him the lowdown on everything. He'd been somewhat bewildered, as he knew about Smythe, naturally. Next morning, I picked him up at the hotel and brought him over to confer with Hammond and Carey, and he was signed to a written contract.

So the Rangers, conscripted by Smythe and shaped by Patrick, made their debut as the home team against the Montreal Maroons on November 17, 1926, about eleven months after the Americans had formally opened the Garden. They did it with the same flair too. Marching bands slipped along the ice, flags hung from the rafters, a movie actress named Lois Moran dropped the ceremonial first puck, and the Rangers made their appearance in blue jerseys with thin red and white stripes before a Wednesday night crowd of 13,000.

The game became so rough that Frank Boucher, who was a gentleman on ice, got into a fight with "Bad Bill" Phillips of the Maroons, who was not. "It was the first and only time I ever had a fight on ice," recalled Boucher, who later won the Lady Byng

For a time, the most popular player in town is Ching Johnson, the bald and amiable roughhouse who skates first for the Rangers and later for the "other" team in the house, the Americans.

Trophy for sportsmanship seven times before the league decided to give it to him permanently. Both players were sent to the penalty box and both paid the price, though it was modest by later yardsticks—$15 apiece.

The price of pugilism wasn't the only novel touch that evening. Between periods, the customary "fancy-skating" demonstration was provided by Katy Schmidt. The referee, Lou Marsh, made his calls with a dinner bell instead of a whistle. And, for a real change, the home team won. The Cook brothers made a family rush on the Montreal goal, and brother Bill banked in the first score for the Rangers in Garden history.

It also was the only score of the night, so the Blues were winners from the start. They kept winning too, and before long began to outdistance the Americans in the standings as well as in the affections of the Garden's high command. After all, the Rangers were the house team; the Amerks were the "other" team. And so a rivalry grew inside the walls. It became a bit unbalanced when the Americans finished the season in fourth place and the Rangers in first. But it thrived because the Americans were generally rakish fellows while the Rangers tended to be more austere in manner, with the notable exception of Ching Johnson, a large and bald hustler on skates who belted opponents with impartial cheerfulness and who soon ranked as the most popular hockey player in town.

Johnson was so popular that he even outdid the extroverts who played for the Americans. But for pranks and social excesses, the finger of suspicion always was pointed at the Americans, and their boss, Tommy Gorman, spent a lot of time defending them in the front office of the Garden. Once, Gorman remembered, he was called in by Colonel Hammond and was lectured about his boys' after-hours activities. At that very moment, the colonel said, they were whooping it up down the block. Gorman, by no means certain that he was doing the right thing, took a pair of security guards from the Garden and hurried outside.

"We located the place on Fifty-first Street," he reported. "Nobody answered our ring, so we hammered on the door. At last it opened, and we walked into a blare of music and the clink of glasses. We found not one of the Americans, but about ten Rangers. They were celebrating Ching Johnson's birthday."

If there was any doubt that the Rangers ruled the roost, it

was dispelled when they ended their second season in the Stanley Cup series in Montreal. They not only won the cup but won it with the "old man" himself guarding the net. They didn't plan it that way; they were forced to extreme measures when the goalie, Lorne Chabot, was struck in the left eye by a flying puck and left the ice on a stretcher. With no other goaltender available, Lester Patrick did the only sane—or probably insane—thing possible. He strapped on Chabot's pads and, at the age of 44, long since retired as an active player, stationed himself in front of the Rangers' goal.

He was still there blocking shots with a 1–0 lead and only six minutes left to play when Nels Stewart scored for Montreal. Then they went into sudden-death overtime, and the white-haired "Silver Fox" became a symbol of resistance even to the roaring crowd. Finally Boucher ripped home the goal that won it for the Rangers and their aging substitute, who was back on the bench running the team a few nights later when they brought the Stanley Cup back to Broadway.

Rickard, who had once questioned the wisdom of staging ice hockey in an arena built for boxing, now had a financial ace up his sleeve, and the Rangers kept the cash flowing even in the Depression days that were gathering. In fact, at the depth of the Depression in 1933, Patrick again steered his Blues to another Stanley Cup championship, and by then he was masterminding a house dynasty. He was later joined by his sons, Lynn and Murray, who also played for the Rangers and coached them. And years afterward, the Rangers sponsored the Lester Patrick Trophy "for outstanding service to hockey."

The "other" team, though, shared neither the profit nor the glory. As the Rangers kept winning games and fans, the Americans kept losing both. Their owner, "Big Bill" Dwyer, left the scene in 1935 after he was convicted of rumrunning. For a time the club was rescued by a defenseman, Red Dutton, whose father owned the Dutton Contracting Business in Canada. The rescue was mostly financial, with the Dutton company bankrolling the team during lean winter days while Red eventually became the coach and manager.

But the ragamuffin Americans enjoyed one howling artistic success before following Big Bill from the hockey scene. On the night of March 27, 1938, they somehow made it to the opening round of the play-offs and found themselves skating against

The Americans don't win many trophies or even games in some years. So when they do, they guard the silverware with promotional zeal. Red Dutton helps keep the team alive in the mid-thirties, though it finally skates off for good in 1942.

their rich cousins, the Rangers. The teams were tied at one game apiece, and this was the deciding game of the two-out-of-three series, with the winner scheduled to advance into the semifinals against Chicago. It was, at long last, a dream match between the Garden's own teams, and it turned into the longest dream in the Garden's hockey history.

For one period nobody scored. Then in the second period, the Rangers scored twice. But in the final period, the Americans scored twice, and they barreled into overtime: whoever scores first, wins it all. But while the crowd of 16,340 raised the roof, they stayed tied through the first overtime period, and through the second, and into the third. By then the arena clocks had slipped past midnight and then past one o'clock in the morning, and the concession stands had run out of food long before the players had run out of energy. And then they struggled through the third period, still deadlocked at 2–2, after playing the equivalent of two full games.

Now the teams came back from their dressing rooms for a seventh period, and the Americans suddenly pieced together one last lunge at Davey Kerr in the Ranger goal. Art Chapman fed a lead pass to Joe Jerwa on the left side. Jerwa passed it to Lorne Carr, who had scored their first goal five periods earlier, and Carr rammed home the shot that finally ended the longest game on Garden ice—120 minutes and 40 seconds of hockey that lasted until 1:25 o'clock in the morning.

But the Americans soon ran out of endurance. When they reached the 1941–42 season, they also ran out of money. The league took over financial responsibility for the team, and one year later they skated for the last time.

After a hockey game at the Garden—but not after *that* hockey game between the Rangers and Americans, which ended five hours after it began—it was customary for the public to inherit the ice. That is, once the players had left, the rink was open to anyone in the audience who cared to put on skates and glide around for a while.

On some evenings, the midnight skaters included a pair of young bachelors who happened to be sportswriters for the *New York Times* and who on some occasions had just covered the game. Occasionally they were joined by a few of the hockey players themselves, and occasionally by a brace of show girls from the stages around the corner. In New York in the Roaring Twenties, nightlife was a way of life, and it started with the new mayor himself, Beau James, his dapper little Honor, Jimmy Walker. The *bons vivants* of the press were James Roach, later the racing writer and sports editor of the *Times*, and Joe Nichols, later the racing writer and chief soloist of the *Times*, who looked back on the gyrating scene afterward and reflected:

The patriarch, Lester Patrick, who not only assembles the original Rangers but also establishes a family dynasty on ice. Later, at the age of 45, he even goes into the nets one night when the team runs short of goaltenders.

Track and field becomes a regular tenant too. Rickard signs Joie Ray, the Chicago taxi driver and distance runner, whose durability carries him from the days of Paavo Nurmi almost to the days of Glenn Cunningham.

There was nothing on the entire sports scene to compare with the mad spectacle of the six-day bicycle race. The colorful, endless whirl of the two-man teams generated almost frenzied enthusiasm among the fans, most of them Europeans, to whom cycling back in their homeland was the prime sport. Foreigners, mostly Italians, predominated among the old contestants, with Franco Georgetti of Milan emerging as the Garden champion through having been on nine victorious teams.

Contrary to popular belief, the cyclists in those races up to 1938 were on the track for every single hour of the event. I saw them at six in the morning as well as at the evening hours of the most strenuous competition.

The unwritten rule, of course, was for the riders to dawdle at the slowest possible pace after the crowd went home following the 2 A.M. sprints, but there was one notable breach of this code. In the 1928 December grind, at 4:30 in the morning, a jam was started by Harry Horan, later a Garden usher. Piqued by one of the more important stars, Horan sprang away from the other riders on the track while only the scorekeepers, the cleaning corps and a few newspapermen looked on.

The furious burst of riding, with all the cast participating, lasted for about a full hour. So unlooked-for and unusual was the outbreak—one full hour of furious jamming before 18,000 empty seats—that the promoter of the race, John Chapman, had to be roused from his room at a nearby hotel to rush over and observe. Most of the riders were angry at Horan, but not Chapman. He put an extra $200 into the pay envelope of the young nonconformist.

It might be argued that anybody who made his living riding a bicycle around an indoor track for six consecutive days and nights was a nonconformist. But that was the essential attraction of the six-day whirl, which became a symbol of the fantasy and the stars and the skills that filled the Garden just as Barnum's acrobats and fire-eaters had done half a century earlier. Not everybody understood the fine points, but everybody understood the broad ones; it was a grind that none of the spectators could share, except vicariously.

They watched Alf Goullet returning year after year to win eight times and, with Alf Grenda, to set an all-time record of 2,758 miles, a mark that still was standing when the races quit the program in 1939. They watched Reggie McNamara lose in 1921 to Goullet, who won thirteen of the final seventeen one-mile sprints to snatch first place. And they watched McNamara win seven bicycle events in two Gardens with six different partners and emerge as the iron man of cycling—an Australian who came to the United States in 1913 and left in 1932 at the age of forty-five with a medical record that included a broken collarbone (four times), a fractured skull (twice), and a cracked rib (twelve times).

For fifteen cents the marveling fan could buy a program that described the life and battles of racing supermen like Torchy Peden of Vancouver, Alf Letourneur of France, Gerard Debaets and Alphonse Goosens of Belgium, and Freddie Spencer, Charley Winter, Carl Stockholm, Cecil Yates, and Goullet of the United States. For a dollar the homeless fan could buy his way into the balcony and pitch his tent for a week, harassed only by fatigue, ushers, and pickpockets.

"Some bike fans literally stayed for the week," remembered Murray Robinson, who covered the event for the *New York World-Telegram*, which later went out of business along with the six-day bicycle race. "You could do it for a dollar admission —if you could live a week without air.

"The pickpockets and coat-snatchers looked forward eagerly to Six-Day Week. Conditions were ideal for gathering boodle in the bedlam. Seasoned bike fans never took off their overcoats. If they did, they went home without them, so fast were they grabbed. The disappearing coats became the subject of a running gag. Peter Prunty, the announcer, would remove his hard hat and begin: 'The 10 o'clock score is—' And a voice from the gallery would call out: 'Forty-three overcoats.' When the pickings were lean, the pickpockets would release balloons among the sleepy fans. When the latter reached up to keep the balloons aloft, their watches, wallets and tie pins disappeared."

Just before dawn, when the Broadway show crowd made its appearance, the bike riders were offered inducements from the crowd—premium cash, known as "premes." Peggy Joyce once posted a cool $1,000 for a sprint, which promptly unfolded while the band played "Pretty Peggy with Eyes of Blue." Mike Delores, "the Mad Hatter of Danbury," raised the ante to $2,400 once. And while they whirled, the imported jazz bands or combos kept the joint jumping and the song pluggers hopping.

Song pluggers were a breed apart, promotional hustlers who created brainstorms to peddle songs. They showed up with their own pianos, which were arrayed inside the infield of the track, and they spent a grueling six nights getting their songs plugged to the public. They got powerful help when the cabarets uptown would close for the night and the jazz bands would promptly head for the Garden, where the action was. "The Memphis Five has just left Harlem," the track announcer would intone at four o'clock in the morning. And moments later: "The Harlem Five has just passed Seventy-second Street."

For the dance marathon, a sort of pedestrian's version of the six-day bike race, Joe Basile and his silver-cornet band regularly trouped in from Newark. And during the New Deal years, the Works Progress Administration obligingly provided its sixty-piece band of Harlem musicians renowned as the Madison Square Garden Syncopators. Still later, after the bands had subsided, Gladys Goodding took charge of the house organ and became a fixed star of whatever event was filling the place.

In fact, she became one of the sounds that the public related to life in the Garden, like Joe Humphreys and his successors as the ring announcers. And in later years, like John Condon—an all-purpose staff officer who might spend all day tending his

desk in the boxing department or running the public-relations department before reviving his energies at the New York Athletic Club and returning to the arena to spend the evening as the public-address voice of the basketball game.

In Gladys Goodding's case, her public role extended beyond the Garden. For years, she played the organ at Ebbets Field by day and then played in the Garden by night. She was a warm, generous woman who lived, for a time, in a hotel near the Garden and who often played music appropriate to the action or the performers. She also inspired a house joke for trivia fans: Who was the only person to play for the Dodgers, Rangers, and Knicks?

The bike riders averaged twelve hours a day apiece, or twenty-four hours a day for each two-man team, and at top speed they hit fifty miles an hour. They were started on their voyage by a pistol fired by celebrity guests like Mayor Walker or his successor, Fiorello La Guardia, or by Al Jolson, Jimmy Durante, Eddie Cantor, Pat O'Brien and Jack Dempsey. After a particularly good day, stars like Peden and McNamara might pocket $1,000 in prize money. They also could sleep for maybe three hours during a particularly good day, though napping in the riders' quarters in the basement became complicated after the management installed a shooting gallery there.

The way of life lost some of its numbing beauty when John Chapman ruled that one week was too long for one admission and imposed a twelve-hour limit on hanging around.

"The all-weekers put up a tough fight," Harry Mendel recalled, as though chronicling the passing of an era. "The cops had to go up and rout them out of the gallery when the twelve hours was up at 6 A.M. and 6 P.M. The mugs would run down to the infield and put up a last stand there."

Four years after Garden III opened, they did chronicle the passing of an era. On January 6, 1929, Tex Rickard suffered an attack of acute appendicitis and died in Miami Beach. But the way of life that he had helped create did not desert him. He was brought back by train to New York aboard the Havana Special in a bronze coffin. He was still flanked by superlatives, too. The casket weighed 2,200 pounds, cost $15,000, and required eighteen policemen and firemen to carry it.

It took thirty-five hours for the procession to reach New

York, where they gave Rickard a parting salute that rivaled most of the events he had staged. His body lay in state in the Garden's arena, covered by a blanket of orchids six feet by fifteen, which his old tiger Jack Dempsey had sent with the message: "My Pal."

For two days the athletes and show people and politicians filed past, maybe 15,000 in all. The final moment of viewing was reserved for Dempsey, who held his top hat tastefully at his side. It was, the press observed, like the rite for "an archbishop in the cathedral he had built."

The Garden, the palace of pleasure, was strict when it came to honoring its heroes or passing its eras. A few years earlier they had held a somewhat more fanciful wake for "John Barleycorn" when the federal government decided to put whiskey to rest. And after Rickard's farewell, sixteen years elapsed before another funeral was permitted there.

The star that time was Sgt. Homer Cook of the United States Marines, who had survived the war but who was killed during the rodeo while trying to mount a wild horse in the chute. It was October 18, 1945, and the next midnight eight cowboys acting as pallbearers placed Cook's coffin on an altar in the center of the Garden, draped in a United States flag. While the rodeo performers filed past, Roy Rogers, the singing cowboy, provided the final flourish with his own rendition of "The Last Roundup."

A box of a building, without the architectural flair of the "palace of pleasure" on Madison Square, but a building reconstructed to provide the busiest stage in New York for 43 years of Depression, prosperity, hot war, cold war and peace.

8 HARD TIMES

"After Tex Rickard died," Harry Markson remembered, "the big fact of life was the Depression. It was difficult to promote anything. Besides, after Jack Dempsey and Gene Tunney, we were blessed with heavyweight champions like Primo Carnera and Max Baer."

Harry Markson was a sportswriter for the *Bronx Home News,* and he stepped into the vacuum after Rickard left the scene and stayed for forty years. He found William F. Carey running the Garden temporarily, and he found Jimmy Johnston running the boxing business there. Johnston, who was from Liverpool, England, was a colorful person known alternately as the Boy Bandit and the Man in the Derby Hat, and for a time he had more nicknames than cash customers.

Even Rickard's legendary "millionaires" were struggling against the hard times caused by the collapse of business in the world's markets. Just before the deluge, in 1927, profits in the Garden climbed beyond a million dollars. Just after the deluge, in 1931, they dwindled to $130,000. A year later, the boxing shows, the pride of the house, netted only $7,000. And a year after that, they took a $59,000 bath.

The Boy Bandit tried to survive the deluge with the help of allies like Francis Albertanti, his press agent, who had witnessed the signing of Benny Leonard and Richie Mitchell in Anne Morgan's drawing room on Madison Avenue a dozen years earlier and who had marveled at Miss Morgan's long cigarette holder and wood-burning fireplace. When Markson encountered him one day in 1933, he discovered that Albertanti was every bit as

In the nineteen-thirties, hard times. But for the Garden, the trumpets of salvation are sounded by a new promoter, Mike Jacobs, and a new heavyweight hero, Joe Louis.

incredulous at the niceties of life outside the boxing ring. The Roaring Twenties had given way to the whimpering Thirties, and the boys on the street were finding it hard to let go.

"I had tickets to a concert by Vladimir Horowitz at Carnegie Hall one night," Markson recalled, reducing the revolution to everyday terms. "But my wife had a cold and couldn't join me. I ran into Albertanti on Broadway. He was a colorful little guy, a legend. I asked him if he was doing anything, and he said he was doing nothing. So I said, let's have dinner. And while we were eating, I said, 'How about coming to Carnegie Hall with me?'

"Albertanti replied, 'What for?' And I said, 'To hear Vladimir Horowitz.' Francis replied, 'Who's that?' And I said, 'The piano player.' And with that, he slammed his steak down on the table as though he'd just heard the world's most outrageous proposition and got up and hustled away. Like he was insulted. And he didn't talk to me for about three weeks."

It was clearly no time for tempting fate by taking any rash new steps, not even to hear a distinguished pianist on a night when no distinguished heavyweight was in town. Even a hardy soul like Franklin D. Roosevelt took the precaution of making amends with the past when he brought his first campaign for the presidency to a climax at the Garden on the evening of November 5, 1932. He got there with Jim Farley, his chief strategist, who recalled later: "It was customary for me to ride with him to Madison Square Garden for the big political meeting we always had a few nights before election. Mr. Roosevelt was a superstitious fellow."

Once inside, Roosevelt found himself surrounded by a solid throng of 22,000 supporters, with 3,000 more outside the Garden behind the police barricades listening to the windup over loudspeakers. His sense of timing proved as sharp as his sense of party loyalty. In a dramatic act of public reconciliation, he threw his arms around Al Smith, who still felt resentful because he had been bypassed four years earlier. And as the two Democratic giants embraced, the crowd stood and roared for eight minutes in a demonstration that filled the air with confetti and that prompted the *New York Times* to concede, with judicious understatement, that the Garden was gripped by "perhaps a little hysteria."

But FDR's appearances were spaced four years apart, and that was stretching the "hysteria" and the rent a little far. The trouble was that people suddenly were confronted with hard choices for their hard money. Movie theaters started giving away bags of groceries and sets of dishes to attract customers. Even in the executive suite, things were growing a bit tense. Colonel Hammond, who had been general manager since Rickard's death, began to blame Carey for the decline of the Garden. And in December 1932, a month after Roosevelt and Smith had brought down the house, the colonel brought the bickering to a peak and resigned.

But it turned out that the old military attaché was merely regrouping. He started to buy stock in the Garden and, within a year and a half, made a strong comeback as part of a new management team that arrived in two stages with the rank of colonel. The spearhead was John Reed Kilpatrick, a member of the board of directors, who became president of the Garden in 1933 and who masterminded things during the hard times of the Depression years and beyond. Kilpatrick came with a full set of athletic credentials and a full chest of campaign ribbons: all-America end on the Yale football team, captain of the track team, Phi Beta Kappa, cavalry sergeant in the Mexican expedition of 1916, staff officer with Gen. John J. Pershing in France, and holder of the Croix de Guerre, the Legion of Honor, and the Distinguished Service Cross.

With Kilpatrick installed as president, it took only a few months for the other colonel, Hammond, to surface as chairman of the board. Then, with the new high command set, all they needed was something to sell. And they got that almost immediately when two uncharted stars appeared, a man with a basketball and a man with a punch.

The basketball was provided by Edward S. "Ned" Irish, a sportswriter for the *New York World-Telegram* who had a degree from the Wharton School of Business and Finance at the University of Pennsylvania and a strange passion for the somewhat low-key sport of college basketball. It was a sport that traced its roots back only forty years or so, and it was still played chiefly in gymnasiums and church basements. But Irish began to wonder about it after he and some other sportswriters were conscripted by Jimmy Walker to stage a series of college tripleheaders for the benefit of the mayor's Unemployment Relief Fund. He wondered because the first of the tripleheaders, held

A newspaperman named Ned Irish joins the cast in 1934 with an idea: college basketball doubleheaders. His first eight events are played before 99,528 customers.

on the last day of 1931, played to a full house, and so did the subsequent games in the next two winters.

By then it was 1934, and Irish was a twenty-nine-year-old man with an obsession. He placed it on the table in the front office of the Garden, where Kilpatrick and Hammond had just formed their alliance, and they hatched a plan with a simple purpose—to fill some of those empty seats with an audience that could afford the tab.

They reinforced the plan with a budget of $25,000 and gave Irish the signal to stage six college basketball doubleheaders. That was good enough for Irish, who quit his newspaper job, even though basketball had been in limbo at the Garden since Rickard had organized the New York Whirlwinds, a professional team led on the court by a five-foot-four-inch whirlwind named Barney Sedran.

They were not nearly so storied or successful as the Original Celtics, a group of pioneers who took the floor with Johnny Beckman, Dutch Dehnert, Pete Barry and, in later years, Nat Holman and Joe Lapchick. But the Whirlwinds were at least the home team in the Garden, though they played their games in relative privacy. For Irish, though, in a time when even pro football was struggling, the chief twist now was that the teams would represent colleges with their built-in followings.

He took the gamble on December 29, 1934, and drew a crowd of 16,188. They watched St. John's take a 14–12 lead at halftime over Westminster, then watched Westminster outscore the local varsity by 25 to 19 in the second half for a 37–33 victory. The leading scorers for St. John's were Rip Kaplinsky and Frank McGuire, later one of the ranking coaches in college basketball. They made eight points apiece. Then, in the "big" game, New York University scored 25 points to 18 for Notre Dame. The officials that night included Frank Lane, who later became famous as a baseball impresario who swung many trades and who once had to be restrained from trading Stan Musial away from the St. Louis Cardinals; Jack Murray, the first manager of the old Whirlwinds; and Pat Kennedy, a dapper little man who became a household god with a rousing act, a no-nonsense whistle, and an unmistakable manner of accusing players of committing fouls.

The opening night proved such a success that two more dates were added to the schedule and, at the end of the winter, the first eight doubleheaders played before 99,528 people. In addition to Notre Dame that season, Irish imported Duquesne, Pittsburgh, Purdue, and Kentucky; and he followed that bit of mass transportation the next winter with North Carolina, Rice, and California. In his third year on the boards, "the Boy Promoter" produced a peak of cross-country frenzy by matching Long Island University against Stanford. It was a classic match, because LIU had a forty-three-game winning streak and Stanford had Hank Luisetti, a radical who fired the ball at the basket one-handed in a Wild West style that entranced the fans and outraged the orthodox coaches. But at the close, Luisetti had fifteen points, Stanford had a 45–31 victory, and LIU had a one-game losing streak.

Two years later, after the season of 1937–38, the regular season was spiced by the first National Invitation Tournament,

But the main draw is the Brown Bomber, who knocks off Paulino Uzcudun in four rounds en route to the title, which he then defends 25 times.

which paired six teams for the "national championship"—Temple, Bradley, NYU, Oklahoma A & M, Colorado, and Long Island. When they got down to the finals, it was Temple against Colorado, with the Philadelphians winning 60–36 over a team that included Byron "Whizzer" White, the all-America football back who later became a Rhodes scholar and still later an associate justice of the United States Supreme Court.

By the time World War II replaced the hard times with tragic times, Ned Irish had proved his point: Basketball, like hockey a decade earlier, was paying its way. By 1943, when Kilpatrick was back on active army duty as a brigadier general, Irish was running the combined show back home as acting president of the Garden. By 1946, when the entire sporting scene began to multiply, pro basketball made a comeback with the New York Knickerbockers and the Basketball Association of America, and this time it stayed.

"Where I come from," Jimmy Cannon observed, bracketing history into two sentences, "basketball was usually the preliminary to a dance. But today professional basketball is a square game and returned to respectability last night at Madison Square Garden."

Somewhere in the depths of the Depression, though, the original art form and the original breadwinner of the Garden—prizefighting—was still waiting for its revival.

Rickard was gone, and so was his main man, Dempsey. So was Gene Tunney, whose only defeat in the ring had come in 1922 at the hands and elbows of Harry Greb, the roughhouse middleweight from Pittsburgh who survived in one of the memorable blood-letting fights in the Garden's history. They knocked heads three times within twenty months in a bruising series, in fact, with Tunney taking a split decision in the second bout and a unanimous decision in the third, and later Tunney beat Greb twice more for good measure. Benny Leonard was gone too, along with Lew Tendler and the other lightweight stars.

So were most of the wrestlers and strongmen who kept the ring alive on the nights when the boxers stayed away. They were good ones, too, going back to the early days of Frank Gotch, who rarely weighed as much as 200 pounds but who lost only six of his 160 bouts before turning his public over to Ed "Strangler"

Lewis, a 270-pounder who lasted thirty-four years, somehow won 6,200 bouts, and banked $4 million. Lewis reached his peak in 1921 and held the world title in wrestling while Dempsey was holding his in boxing. Then he gave way to Jim Londos, "the Golden Greek," who lost fourteen times in a row to the Strangler before turning the tables one night in Chicago before a crowd of 32,265, when Lewis was forty-four years old.

By then it was 1934, and the fight mob was as hungry for new heroes as the veterans' army was hungry for jobs. Only the echoes remained, including the echoes of the great old ring announcer Joe Humphreys, whose Victorian prose had accompanied the business from the days of river barges to the days of Rickard's ring. When he was not leading the mob in "Auld Lang Syne" on sentimental occasions, Humphreys was providing a show within a show, introducing the "contestants" in his measured phrases or silencing the galleries with his admonition "Quiet, please, quiet."

When Jack Sharkey fought Max Schmeling in 1930, a low blow ended the fight at the end of round four. At least, a low blow by Sharkey at the end of round four gave the fight—and Sharkey's heavyweight title—to Schmeling, either at the end of round four or the beginning of round five, when Schmeling was physically unable to answer the bell. The distinction was no mere footnote to heavyweight history, not if you had any money riding on the fateful round. But Humphreys, standing as usual like an oak tree in the center of the confusion within the ring, announced in a commanding manner that the fight was considered finished when the round was finished, not later.

At ringside, Graham McNamee leaned into his microphone and, sensing the cash significance of the judgment, reported to his radio audience:

"Well, that clears that up. In other words, any of you boys who happen to have a dollar or so on this case, the knockout, according to Joe Humphreys, the demon announcer, took place in the fourth round, not the fifth."

When Humphreys passed from the scene as the sonorous voice of New York boxing six years later, his funeral cortege was directed down Eighth Avenue past the Garden in the same sort of flamboyant farewell that the boys had contrived for Rickard. Nobody sang "Auld Lang Syne" that time, but the next year the boxing writers hung a plaque on the wall of the Garden to me-

During the Joe Louis years, two partners run the show: Mike Jacobs (left) handles the fights and Gen. John Reed Kilpatrick handles everything else.

morialize Joe's contributions. And, for old times' sake, before the ceremony they sat down to a beefsteak dinner in the Garden.

To keep the line intact, Joe was succeeded as "the voice" by Harry Balogh, a genius at delivering ad-lib remarks and off-the-cuff speeches. Balogh kept the faith too. He reached the pinnacle of achievement in filling empty time one night when he received an urgent appeal from the management to delay the proceedings in the ring. It was no simple task to conduct a filibuster over a public-address system. But, in the best style of his late, lamented predecessor, he launched into a meandering monologue about nothing in particular and kept it going until he closed it splendidly by intoning:

"And in conclusion, may I extend to you my best wishes . . . for a happy and enjoyable . . . *Memorial Day.*"

But regardless of the quality of the language inside the ring, the Garden still lacked quality of *performance* inside the ring. They desperately needed a man with a punch. As Harry Markson recalled later:

> You had a lot of fighters and activity in those days, but not much money. Everything was on the downside.
>
> But late in 1933, something happened. Three of the top sports people for the Hearst newspapers were staging fights in those days for Mrs. Hearst's Free Milk Fund for Babies. They were Damon Runyon, the columnist; Ed Frayne, the sports editor of the *New York American;* and Bill Farnsworth, the sports editor of the *Journal.* They were putting on the fights in the Garden Bowl, which had been built by the Garden a couple of years earlier in Long Island City for outdoor bouts. Then the Garden raised their rent a bit, maybe by 10 percent or 12½ percent. So these three guys decided to form their own outfit.
>
> They called it the Twentieth Century Sporting Club, and they hired a ticket seller named Mike Jacobs as their promoter. Mike had helped Tex Rickard underwrite the Dempsey-Carpentier fight on Boyle's Thirty Acres in Jersey. He had gone through the third grade in school maybe, but he was a shrewd businessman. He once paid Enrico Caruso $10,000 a night for a tour of the country, singing, and Mike made like $80,000 on it.
>
> Anyway, on January 24, 1934, they put on their first fight. Billy Petrolle against Barney Ross, the lightweight champion, in a nontitle bout at the Bronx Coliseum. They were in business.
>
> Then they heard about this kid fighting in Chicago, a young heavyweight who was knocking guys out with both hands. His name was Joe Louis. So Mike grabbed a train to Chicago and met with the two men who were handling the kid, John Roxborough

and Julian Black. He explained that he wanted to bring Louis to New York, and they asked him, "What do we have to do?" Mike answered, "Win as fast as you can. In the first round, if you can."

In those days, black fighters took orders. So this was a novelty, what he'd just told them, so Roxborough and Black told Jacobs, "You're our man." They signed with Mike, and Joe Louis came to New York.

Madison Square Garden was not too troubled by the fact that Jacobs had locked up the heavyweight prodigy for the rival Twentieth Century Sporting Club, and there was a simple reason for the indifference: The Garden was busy promoting the heavyweight title fight between Max Baer and James J. Braddock. It took place outdoors in the Garden Bowl on June 13, 1935, with Braddock lifting the title in spite of 10-to-1 odds that said he had no chance. But the fight was no financial coup; the gate totaled only $205,366.

Twelve days later, in Yankee Stadium, the new boys on the promotional block unveiled Joe Louis, who not only knocked out Primo Carnera but also outdrew the Garden's title fight where it counted, in the till. And Louis, finishing the job in six rounds, minded his "orders" seriously: "Win as fast as you can."

Joe Louis Barrow, twenty-one years old, seventh child of a sharecropping family from Alabama, had been a professional for exactly one year and his record now read: 23 victories in a row, 19 by knockouts. Six weeks later, with Jacobs still dangling him in front of the boxing Establishment, he tapped out King Levinsky in the first round in Chicago. Then, six weeks after that, he overpowered a reluctant Max Baer in the fourth. Now Jacobs was ready to play his ace, Harry Markson recalled:

Mike took over boxing at the Hippodrome, which was the Radio City Music Hall of its day. It was at Sixth Avenue and Forty-third Street, only a few blocks from the Garden. But then Jacobs put it all together. He had a hall and he had a fighter, and pretty soon he had the Garden. He began by renting the Garden for two Joe Louis fights. The first one was on December 13, and Joe took out Paulino Uzcudun in four rounds. The second one was early in 1937, and Joe won a ten-round decision over Bob Pastor. But in between he had knocked out six other guys, and a few months later he kayoed Braddock in Chicago for the title.

So now he had the heavyweight champion, too. And so, on the ancient theory that you join 'em if you can't lick 'em, the Garden decided to embrace Mike Jacobs. In the fall of 1937, they took him in—signed him to a contract to promote fights on a rental basis for two years. But after one year, they tore up the contract and signed a 50-50 deal. They became full partners on everything, expenses and losses and profits. It lasted from 1937 until the spring of 1949. By then, Louis had defended his title twenty-five times.

In the twenties, Rickard had Dempsey. In the thirties and forties, Jacobs had Louis. And in the fifties, after the International Boxing Club took over, Jim Norris had Rocky Marciano. But the important thing was that boxing was revived.

It was revived, all right. Along the way, Jacobs brought in a machine from St. Louis named Henry Armstrong, who won the world featherweight title in 1937 in the first Garden bout promoted by the Twentieth Century Sporting Club and who later won the lightweight and welterweight titles—and held all three at the same time.

In 1941 Fritzie Zivic took away the welterweight title by knocking out Henry in the twelfth round of a bruising fight watched by a record Garden crowd of 23,306. But the pipeline was loaded with talent by then. In one of the preliminaries that night, the fight mob got its first look at a young welterweight named Walker Smith. He was a man with devastating skills who fought 202 times and lost only 9 times, who held the middleweight championship 5 times, and who reigned as perhaps the best in the business for a quarter of a century as Sugar Ray Robinson.

"The fight tomorrow night," Jimmy Cannon once wrote in the poetical prose that portrayed the man and the era, "suggests a solo by Robinson instead of an athletic contest. The result will be judged by what Robinson does. It will be his failure or triumph."

If there was any doubt that prizefighting had risen out of the ashes of the hard times, it was dispelled during one month in 1944 by a young lightweight from Georgia named Beau Jack. On March 3 he lost his title to Bob Montgomery. On March 17 he returned to the scene and defeated Al "Bummy" Davis. And on March 31 he won a decision from the National Boxing Association champion, Juan Zurita. Each time he performed, he was watched by a capacity crowd.

"Beau Jack sold out the Garden three times in one month," Harry Markson said, reducing things to their simplest terms. "How's that for bringing in the public?"

Even Tex Rickard would have raised an eyebrow over that one.

That's right, basketball on skates. In an earlier time, they used to entertain the spectators between periods with "fancy skating" exhibitions.

When Glenn Cunningham was eight years old, his legs were burned so severely in a school fire in Kansas that doctors wondered if he would ever walk normally again. So, in the perverse manner of people with a single purpose, he started to run—so that he might walk.

By 1933 he was running so far so fast that he was being referred to as the Iron Horse. During the next seven years, Cunningham brought his act into the Garden every winter and—at a time when basketball was being born as an attraction and boxing was being reborn—he became the pacemaker of waves of track-and-field athletes who otherwise might have spent the years between the Olympic Games in obscurity.

High-jumpers like Cornelius Johnson joined the lists, along

with sprinters like Ben Johnson of Columbia, middle-distance runners like Joe McCluskey of Fordham, long-distance runners like Greg Rice of Notre Dame, and pole-vaulters like Cornelius Warmerdam, who astonished the world in 1942 by clearing fifteen feet in the days before fiberglass poles. And gallery fans crowded the railings of the upper balcony for a glimpse of Emil Von Elling's relay teams from NYU.

But the magic distance remained the mile—eleven laps around the boards. And Cunningham led a pack of runners that included Gene Venzke, Joe Mangan, Archie San Romani, Chuck Fenske, Bill Bonthron and, later, Gil Dodds and Leslie Mac-Mitchell. One night in 1935, during the Knights of Columbus Games, he defeated Chuck Hornbostel at 1,000 yards and took two seconds off the world record, then came back ninety minutes later to beat Venzke at the mile. Another time, he chased Jimmy Herbert to a world record at 600 yards and then returned later and lowered the world record for the mile to 4:07.4.

Then there was the night in 1936 when he got into a slow-pace duel with Venzke and Mangan until the last two laps, when everybody began to sprint home. The winner was Cunningham, but the time was a tortoiselike 4:46.4. And, because newspaper readers the next day had trouble believing their eyes, the race became known as the Typographical Error Mile.

Cunningham and his crowd appeared a generation before the four-minute miles of Roger Bannister and his crowd in the post-war years. But they made familiar terms of things like the Baxter Mile, the Millrose Games, the New York Athletic Club meet, the Knights of Columbus Games, and the Wanamaker Mile. Like Beau Jack, they played to full houses. And when they passed from the scene, having created another indoor specialty, Jesse Abramson considered the milestones that Cunningham had raced past and wrote: "In his eight years as a Garden participant, no one could match Cunningham's achievements, records, consistency, range, and impact."

The statistics matched the words. In thirty-one appearances in the Garden in either the mile or the 1,500 meters, the rehabilitated man from Kansas won twenty-one races and finished second in six others. He won the Wanamaker Mile six times, the NYAC mile five times, and the Knights of Columbus mile six times. Not even Joie Ray and Pietri Dorando had *that* in their files.

Sometimes they even build a ski jump inside the arena, from the rafters to the rink below.

Maurice Richard, the "Rocket" of the Montreal Canadiens, leans on the Rangers for years. He's applying the muscle here to Edgar Paprade in 1950.

By the time John Reed Kilpatrick and a lot of other people began reaching for their army uniforms, business was brimming in the old trolley barn. In the old days, when things were really rough, the Garden was occupied maybe 30 percent of the time. But now the stage was being set and reset every day, sometimes twice a day for afternoon basketball games and evening hockey games. And in a typical week, the schedule might look like this:

Monday: tennis matches, attendance of 12,371.
Tuesday: hockey game, 11,125.
Wednesday: basketball doubleheader, 16,439.
Thursday: hockey again, 6,392.
Friday: fight night, 12,801.
Saturday: firemen's dance, 20,000.

There were a few forgettable nights, but not too many. In 1935 they tried an animated bridge tournament, with the ushers walking around the arena displaying huge models of playing cards for the enlightenment of the audience—which numbered only 522 persons. They tried indoor dancing and dropped

Men at work: Duncan Fisher of the Rangers fires, but Frank Brimsek of the Chicago Black Hawks blocks the shot and gets plenty of support.

$100,000. Indoor soccer was offered, with four teams of seven players apiece, but only 8,000 customers showed up for the experiment, which reached a peak of excitement when several of the players got into a brawl. They even tried girls' softball, lacrosse, and the Women's International Exhibition of Arts and Industries.

The Coldstream Guards and the Bolshoi Ballet lent an international and cultural tone, which moved the impresario Sol Hurok to observe, "We were able to create a new public by using the Garden."

The new public was there on the evening of May 25, 1939, to hear the great pianist Ignace Paderewski, who had played in Stanford White's old Garden forty-eight years earlier. Now the master was seventy-eight years old, and a remarkable crowd of 18,000 filled the arena as he arrived in a limousine and disappeared into a special dressing room that had been built on the stage.

They waited, and waited some more. Meanwhile, inside the dressing room, Paderewski was struggling against something that the house's boxers and hockey players could understand—a chill. It rippled through his body and numbed his fingers. He rubbed his hands, he soaked them in warm water, and the crowd waited respectfully in the rows of seats. But none of the ministrations worked. The recital was called off and the money was refunded.

On that occasion, at least, an exceptionally novel entry was made in the diary: Paderewski concert scratched because of cold fingers. But with Joe Louis, Sugar Ray Robinson, Glenn Cunningham, Hank Luisetti, and Beau Jack taking up the slack, the Garden solved most of its problems and drew clear of the decade of hard times. And in January 1941, a winter of war, the management staged an event of its own. The building's old $3 million mortgage was torn to shreds and ceremonially burned—in the Stanley Cup, which the Rangers had obligingly brought home nine months earlier.

But the war that was already engulfing Europe was casting shadows across the Atlantic, and the meeting halls of America were becoming the battlegrounds of the political conflicts of the war.

One of the most typical and clamorous events in this political struggle took place at the Garden on Friday evening, May 23,

Sonja Henie, once the child star of the
Olympics, dazzles them on skates for a
generation. Her partners run the full range,
from Jimmy Cannon, the sports columnist
and chronicler, to Harrison Thomson, who
evidently skates for a living in formal whites.

Political rallies, too. Charles A. Lindbergh, the pioneering pilot, takes the rostrum to plead for America First during the countdown to World War II.

1941, just six months before the attack on Pearl Harbor. The event was a mass meeting of the America First Committee, and the chief speaker was Charles A. Lindbergh, the pioneering pilot and national hero, who was now trying to rally public opinion against President Roosevelt's foreign policy, specifically to keep the United States from involvement in the war.

The doors to the Garden were opened at 5 o'clock that evening, and within an hour, crowds were streaming into the arena. By 7:30, most of the seats were filled. Five minutes later, when the throng opened the rally by singing "America," there were 20,000 persons inside and perhaps 14,000 outside listening while loudspeakers carried the program into the streets surrounding the Garden. Both inside and outside, 800 policemen worked to keep order.

At 8:27, the Fire Department ordered the doors closed, and three minutes later, Lindbergh arrived and made his way to the platform with Norman Thomas, the Socialist leader, and Kathleen Norris, the novelist. The ovation lasted five minutes, and then the crowd sat back to hear the headline speeches by Lindbergh and Senator Burton K. Wheeler of Montana.

"The audience," the *New York Times* reported, "was highly demonstrative and noisy, breaking into speeches with repeated outbursts of applause for every statement that America wants to keep out of war, for every mention of Mr. Lindbergh, Senator Wheeler and other isolationist leaders, for all isolationist slogans and for all assertions that the United States is strong and mighty enough not to worry about its defense from any invader, even if Britain falls and the British fleet is taken over by Hitler."

9 THE MAIN EVENT

From June 1, 1945, to June 1, 1946, while a new generation of Johnnies came marching home from war, the American public threw itself into peace with a passion, as it had done a quarter of a century earlier. And in that corner of the world a block off Broadway where the turnstiles began clicking again, an army marched through the doors during the twelve months when the boom started—5,298,544 in all.

"Madison Square Garden," observed the columnist Bugs Baer, echoing the words of the observers of past generations, "became the terminal for all whose talents were unusual and whose services were unique."

The "terminal" in this case came in many dimensions, depending on the particular talents and services on display. For stage shows, the arena was fitted with a platform 4½ feet high, 10 feet deep, and anywhere from 40 to 60 feet across the footlights. For boxing, the "squared circle" measured 24 by 24, rising 43 inches above the ringside seats.

For basketball, wooden panels were placed on the floor like a giant jigsaw puzzle, 104 sections of clear-grain white pine forming a court 100 feet long and 57 feet wide. At each end, new glass backboards were raised, 3 by 6 feet, with mesh baskets 10 feet above the floor; and if you banked the ball into the basket, it bounced off glass three-quarters of an inch thick.

For hockey, the arena was flooded and frozen over. It was 16,000 square feet—well, 15,810 to be exact—and the rink stretched 186 feet the long way and 85 feet across, with goals 6 feet wide and 4 deep, and ice half an inch thick.

The postwar boom brings professional basketball onto the scene, with stars like Carl Braun of the New York Knicks, who lets fly a one-hander. Behind him, one of the early giants of the sport: George Mikan of the Minneapolis Lakers.

Opposite:
But no giant stands taller, or jumps higher, than Wilt Chamberlain. His Philadelphia Warriors teammate Paul Arizin, No. 11, watches Wilt doing his thing. The result: 54 points against the Knicks.

For indoor track, 80 sections of spruce were placed in an oval pattern, 6 feet wide and 12 long for each section, 11 laps to the mile. On the straightaway, the track was 16 feet wide, and it could even handle the 60-yard dash, though the dashers ended their sprint in the lobby, and with a little hard luck might have ended on Eighth Avenue.

For everything under the roof, the main arena extended 240 feet 7 inches from one end to the other and 109 feet 10 inches across, an area of 30,000 square feet. It was, what the plaque on the Fiftieth Street wall still proclaimed, "Dedicated to Athletics, Amusements and the Industrial Arts."

During the twelve months' transition from war to peace, the giant stage was crammed with the following events and spectators.

Boxing. Forty-six professional events drew 558,950 customers; the Golden Gloves amateur bouts, 18,355; the intercity Golden Gloves, 19,246; the Tournament of Champions, 18,659. Only two title fights helped the stampede. Willie Pep kept his featherweight championship against Phil Terranova, and Marty Servo won the welterweight crown from the recent GI, Freddie "Red" Cochrane. The biggest gate was drawn for Rocky Graziano and Servo; it totaled 19,088. The fight lasted two rounds, until Graziano scored by a knockout.

Basketball. All things to all men, basketball drew the following audiences:

    21 college doubleheaders—380,346
    National Invitation Tournament—73,894
    NCAA regionals and finals—55,302
    12 high school afternoons—94,285
    East-West All-Star Game—18,157
    Red Cross charity game—6,734
    All 42 dates on the court—628,718

Hockey. The Rangers, playing to standing-room-only crowds almost every time they were on the ice, drew 387,335 to 25 games. The Rovers, the amateur home team, drew 199,355 to 21.

Ice Shows. They had begun as entertainment between the periods of hockey games at a $2 top. But now Sonja Henie and her Hollywood Revue skated before 206,771 customers in 15 shows, her ninth annual visit. And in all nine years, the "Golden Girl" and Olympic champion drew 1,310,000. Shipstad & John-

The changeover: like a huge jigsaw puzzle, the arena is converted from basketball to hockey in the few hours from the matinee to the evening's performance.

Joe Lapchick, an alumnus of the Original Celtics, takes charge of the Knicks in their second season and leads them through league mergers into the National Basketball Association.

son's Ice Follies, making it for the tenth year, attracted 160,407 persons for 15 shows.

Circus. It held the stage for 77 dates during the year, the most for any event on the calendar. And it drew 928,342 people, the most for any event.

Rodeo. For 33 performances in the heart of Manhattan, it played before 493,867, offered $150,000 in prizes, and included 250 cowboys from Texas, New Mexico, Oklahoma, Idaho, Wyoming, and Montana for "the world championships."

Track. Eight meets held, 83,815 admissions counted.

One-Night Stands. Balls, benefits, political rallies, union mass meetings, religious and social conclaves—36 dates in all and 798,462 paying persons.

Exposition Hall. Events in the basement. For the Sportsmen's Show, the Antiques Show, the Poultry, Dog, and Cat shows, and you name it: 167,544.

But as Shakespeare suggested, by their stars you shall know them—not necessarily by their numbers, not even when their numbers reached 5,298,544 in one year. Just before the war, the star system stretched from Joe Louis in the prize ring to My Own Brucie in the show ring—the heavyweight champion and the cocker spaniel champion of 1940 and 1941; and in the postwar years, from Rocky Marciano to a double-winning Doberman pinscher, Champion Rancho Dobe's Storm.

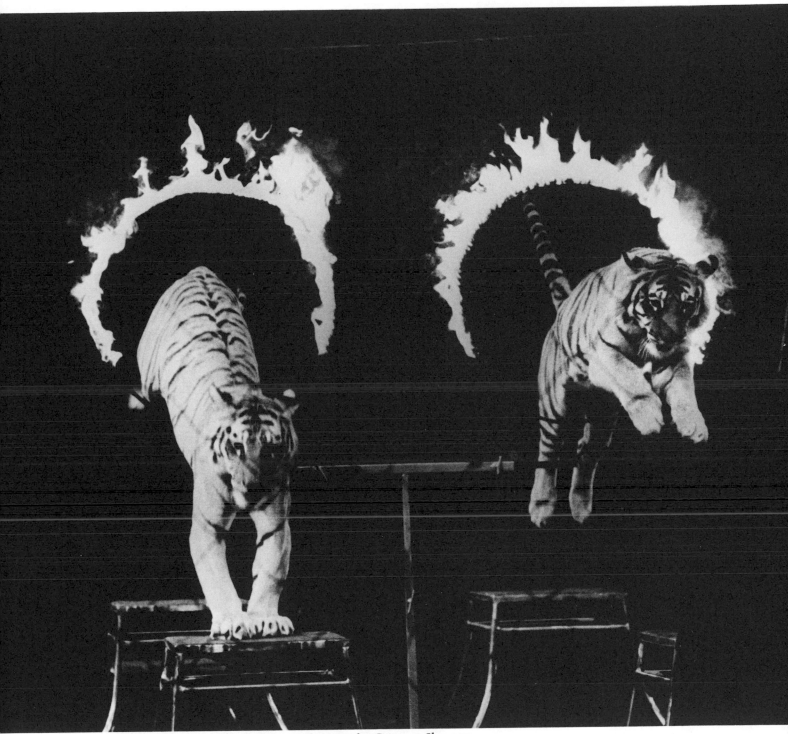

As it was in Barnum's day, and in Barnum's phrase, "the Greatest Show on Earth." It returns every year for a century as the surest sign of spring. . . .

It returns with new acts but also the old standbys: flying acrobats, charging chariots, trained elephants and stunting daredevils.

They manage some neat tricks in the Ice Follies, too: skating in formation, even paddling a canoe.

The stars included a new generation of basketball players and coaches, too. Howard Cann coached New York University's teams for thirty-five seasons, and his 1933–34 team was the first unbeaten one in the city in twenty-five years. Nat Holman, a high school teammate of "Jake" Cann, coached for City College for thirty-seven seasons, losing 188 games but winning 422 and in 1950 steering the first team ever to championships in both the National Invitation Tournament and the National Collegiate Association of America tournament. Clair Bee coached at Long Island University through winning streaks of 43 games and 34 games, took the NIT in 1939 and again in 1941, and ran up a record of 223 victories against only 20 losses in the seven years before the war.

Then there was Joe Lapchick, whose twenty years at St. John's produced four NIT titles and whose nine years with the professionals marked the start of an era that led to the seven-foot center and the $400,000 salary.

But it seemed to many people during the boom year of 1945–46 that the one electric moment in the Garden belonged to a skinny, 140-pound guard from Rhode Island who made one virtuoso performance, probably one virtuoso shot, that symbolized the headlong rush. His name was Ernie Calverley, and he had his memorable fling on March 14, 1946, in the opening round of the ninth NIT.

The Rhode Island team took the floor as a 12-point underdog to Bowling Green and its tall center, Don Otten, a marvel in those days at 6 feet 11½ inches. But the rushing Rhode Islanders tied the score fourteen times during the game and, with only three seconds left to play, were trailing, 74–72. Even when one of their players was fouled, they seemed to have no chance of surviving. But, waiving the one free throw under the rules, they took the ball out of bounds. Suddenly Calverley took the pass and, as time ran out, let fly a two-handed shot on the run. It climbed almost out of sight toward the rafters, arched down through the smoke, and swished through the basket as the final buzzer was drowned in the roar of 18,548 fans. Tape-measure distance: 55 feet.

Matty Begovich, the referee, remembered, "At first, I didn't think it would reach the foul line." But the ball kept rising and finally dropped straight through, the most legendary two points of the 1,868 that Calverley scored in his college career. They were so legendary that most people probably forgot that Rhode Island went on to upset Bowling Green in overtime and even reached the finals, before losing the tournament to Kentucky by one point.

Three months later, in a quieter setting, more basketball history was made during a meeting at the Commodore Hotel. It was directed by a New Haven lawyer named Maurice Podoloff, who also was president of the American Hockey League, and it was called to form a new professional basketball league, the Basketball Association of America. It cast a long shadow into an era when pro basketball would become high-powered and high-priced entertainment, and the eleven charter members of the association cast some long shadows too.

They were the Boston Celtics, the Philadelphia Warriors, the Chicago Stags, the Pittsburgh Ironmen, the Cleveland Rebels, the Washington Capitols, the Detroit Falcons, the Providence Steamrollers, the St. Louis Bombers, the Toronto Huskies, and the New York Knickerbockers. They wanted the Knicks there, understandably, because of the Garden. But even before one basketball was bounced, it became clear that the Garden already had been preempted by the colleges with their sold-out houses, and only half a dozen playing dates were still open.

So the Knicks switched downtown for their twenty-four other home games and camped inside the Sixty-ninth Regiment Armory at Lexington Avenue and Twenty-third Street, not far from the old railroad shed where Barnum's circus had taken residence three-quarters of a century before. They had only 5,000 seats there, and they had trouble filling even those. But, scrounging for talent, the new team in town turned to the only logical place, the colleges.

From Manhattan College, they came up with Neil Cohalan as the coach; from Princeton, John "Bud" Palmer; from Rhode Island, Stan Stutz; from City College, Sonny Hertzberg; from NYU, Ralph Kaplowitz; from LIU, Ossie Schechtman; from NYU and Princeton, Bill van Breda Kolff; and from Purdue, a six-foot-six-inch center, Forest Weber.

They launched the new league on November 1, 1946, by beating the Huskies at Toronto, 68 to 66. And a week and a half later, they took the floor for the first time in the Garden, drawing 17,205 fans and losing to the Chicago Stags in overtime. But they averaged fewer than 12,000 for the six games in the Garden, which were preceded by prelims that featured Industrial League games—Gimbels, Abraham & Straus, and the Metropolitan Life Insurance Company—or the Greater Metropolitan Girls' Basketball League.

When the winter ended—a long one at that—the Knicks had won 33 games and lost 27, and they stood third in the Eastern Division, 16 games behind the Washington Capitols, coached by Red Auerbach, who later led the Celtics to nine championships as the premier power of pro basketball. But the BAA dropped half a million dollars in its first season, and then dropped the Toronto, Pittsburgh, and Cleveland clubs.

By then the Knicks had a new coach, Joe Lapchick, plus a greater beachhead in the Garden. And by 1949 they had a new league. It was formed by the merger of nine teams from the rival National Basketball League into the Basketball Association of America. They included the Minneapolis Lakers with George Mikan, a six-foot-ten-inch center who promptly gave pro basketball its first towering star. The result: the National Basketball Association.

If the pros needed any further shove toward the public favor and purse, they got it from a sad source—a gambling scandal that shattered Nat Holman, ripped apart his City College team after its greatest success, and undermined amateur basketball.

It surfaced a year after Holman's team had finished the 1949–50 season with a record of 17 and 5, thereby earning a bid to the National Invitation Tournament as an underdog. The team startled the country by roaring through four of the best college teams in the land: San Francisco, the defending NIT champion; Kentucky, the defending NCAA champion; Duquesne; and Bradley, the nation's top-ranked squad.

Having climbed to that unlikely peak, the Beavers then earned a spot in the NCAA tournament. To almost all observers except those who chanted "Allagaroo-garoo-garaa" during their games, they had also probably earned a fast downfall. But no. They edged past Ohio State by one point, took North Carolina by five, and finally upset Bradley by three for the second time in a week of postseason history. And so Holman and his playground whiz kids reached the pinnacle, where no other college team had ever stood. They were winners of both major championships in the same year.

Three players stood tallest on that team, figuratively speak-

Under the basket, the Knicks struggle against the powerhouse: the Boston Celtics. No. 6 is the main man, Bill Russell.

ing: Irv Dambrot, Ed Warner, and Ed Roman. They scored 58 points in the NIT final against Bradley, then scored 41 in the NCAA final against Bradley. But one year later, their victories —and much of the glory of college basketball—were swamped by the scandal.

The mean facts were these: thirty-two players from seven colleges were implicated in "shaving" the points in eighty-six games in twenty-three cities and seventeen states. They included players from Manhattan, NYU, Long Island, and the two tournament finalists, Bradley and City College. Much of the blame was directed at the gamblers who openly worked their trade in the biggest arenas, like the Garden, which switched its emphasis and affection after that to the professionals.

It took time and talent to restore the glitter that the colleges had found and then lost, but in time the talent appeared. It appeared most memorably on the night of January 9, 1958, when the University of Cincinnati arrived with a six-foot-five-inch sophomore named Oscar Robertson. Seton Hall scored 54 points that night, but Oscar scored 56, which was more than anybody had ever poured through the baskets, amateur or pro.

Two years later, Richie Guerin of the Knicks went Oscar one better, scoring 57 points against the Syracuse Nationals. One year later, Elgin Baylor of the Los Angeles Lakers scored 71 against the Knicks. And two years after that, Wilt Chamberlain of the Philadelphia Warriors scored 73 in a game against the Knicks. The Knicks did have one consolation. Eight months earlier, in a nightmare at Hershey, Pennsylvania, the remarkable Wilt had totaled an even 100 points against them. So at least they were getting the idea.

Backstage at the Garden, a small army of engineers, carpenters, and production people worked 365 days each year to construct the stages that the stars of the show took over for their acts.

One of the officers of the army was Dick Donopria, a civilized, pipe-smoking man who joined the staff in 1932 from a consulting-engineering firm and who stayed to become superintendent of the entire plant. He wasn't concerned so much with basketball players who scored or shaved points as with the day-to-day labors it required to bring them before their public. He was the chief stage-setter on the premises.

186

Sometimes his problems were somewhat obscure, and he faced them in the middle of the night when the house was empty except for the work crews. He encountered a problem like that on his first night on the job as the number-one solver of problems; when the glass backboards for the basketball court were uncrated, they came out in pieces. Somehow they had been cracked, and now, while the carpenters were fitting the floor panels together for the next evening's game, Dick Donopria found himself with two shattered glass backboards.

It was two o'clock in the morning. Even if you could buy such items in a sporting-goods store, none was open. Where in the world *do* you come up with glass backboards on demand? Uncertain, but also undismayed, he got into his car and drove crosstown to the Hippodrome, where Mike Jacobs was promoting boxing, basketball, and sideshows like jai alai, and he kept poking around the building until he found a set of delivery doors that weren't locked. Once inside, he hunted down the night watchman and exerted a little in-the-trade diplomacy, and the next night the boys were shooting at a pair of borrowed—but unbroken—glass backboards.

The only adventure like that one, Donopria remembers, that couldn't be solved on time involved the six-day bicycle race. Great precision was needed in piecing the banked track together, and the job was usually turned over to a private contractor. But this time the contractor worked his way into a corner and found himself with no boards that could be curved *or* banked at the far ends. There they were, trapped with a gigantic jigsaw puzzle as the clock ticked toward show time.

It ticked past show time too, and the start of the race had to be delayed until three o'clock in the morning. But six-day bike riders are a hardy breed, to say nothing of the people who pay to stay and watch.

"People stuck around," Donopria reasons, "because they were more fascinated watching the carpenters fitting the track together than they would have been watching the bike races."

When presidents of the United States made the scene instead of bicycle riders, the problems naturally multiplied.

One of the staff officers involved in that problem was John Goldner, another deliberate type who was hired in 1936 by Ned Irish as an office boy. Goldner had graduated from NYU four years earlier, but this was the Depression and nobody was sneezing at any job, even a seasonal one that lasted from December to March while basketball players were following a schedule that did not then spill over into the late spring.

By the time he was a year-round executive in the place, Goldner had a private office, a Viking beard, and a title—assistant to the vice-president for productions. He also had the job of getting presidents in and out of the building with no complications. But it wasn't easy.

"When the President was scheduled to appear," Goldner recalls, "you had to give the Secret Service people the names of every person working that night—engineering department people, concession workers, ushers, everybody. And the Secret Service would check them all out to spot guys with past incidents of any kind or to siphon off any potential troublemakers. They usually found none, but they were meticulous."

Once, though, the Secret Service repaid Goldner for his cooperation. President Eisenhower was expected in the Garden, and a zealous White House staff member instructed Goldner to erect a fifty-foot canopy over the entrance for the President. He was still puzzling that one over, but determined to comply, when he mentioned the order to one of the Secret Service chiefs in the advance party. He was advised to forget the canopy, which he did, with thanks.

Sometimes the problems were subtle, like the night years earlier when Paderewski came down with the chill and wasn't able to give his piano recital. The Garden had taken elaborate pains for the aged master, even providing a ramp so that his limousine could drive inside the building to the platform-stage itself. After that, he had to walk only three steps to the private dressing room that had been provided. But he was still too sick to go on, despite the precautions.

"I always wondered," Donopria says with a scholarly interest in the problem, "whether Paderewski was bothered by the fresh aluminum paint on the walls of his dressing room and the stage. You never know where the trouble will be."

The political tinge of the show never concerned the staff army as much as the logistics. In the old days, rallies and benefits were common in the Garden. They would range, politically speaking, from Mme. Chiang Kai-shek all the way to the Communist party.

"If it was somebody as famous as Madame Chiang," Donopria remembers, "we just never got home, we were so busy setting things up. Still, you don't have benefits anymore. They were a thing of the past. Maybe television changed all that. I don't know, but in the old Garden you always had about three Communist meetings a week. The old saying was: If you have a dark day with no show, call the party and they'll come running."

When the crisis centered on animals instead of people, it could be a horse of another color. Sometimes a panther of another color.

The longest-running show on the floor every year was the circus; ten weeks every spring, with time out for eight basketball or hockey games, one-night stands dropped into the schedule. That required eight fast changeovers of the arena, but that wasn't the crisis; that took only a few hours and not much head-scratching.

It also was no great chore to install the circus in the first place. As Donopria puts it, "We just get our junk out of the way, and the circus people bring in their own equipment, performers, and animals."

The circus brought in about 250 people, who lived on their own train in the railroad yards on the West Side of Manhattan. When they moved into the Garden, it took them only about eight or ten hours to set up their rigging and place their mats over the cement floor. When they removed their trappings for a hockey game, they simply raised the rigging away from the spectators' sight lines, took up the rubber mats from the floor, and got out of the way while the Garden crews froze the rink. About an hour later: the face-off.

The animals, meanwhile, were housed in the rotunda of the Garden, and they were rather unusual as house pets go: twenty or more elephants, forty horses, a llama or two and a giraffe or two, a pair of camels, fifteen lions, and twenty tigers, plus maybe an exotic creature like a black panther.

"We get out of their way," Donopria says, with understandable deference, "and let them bring in their own acts."

Sometimes the acts played before an empty house, which was probably fortunate. One time a trainer wanted to practice his routine while the circus was moving in, and his black panther escaped from the cage. The beast was lured back after a short stroll around the floor, during which the work crews scattered as though someone had tripped the air-raid alarm.

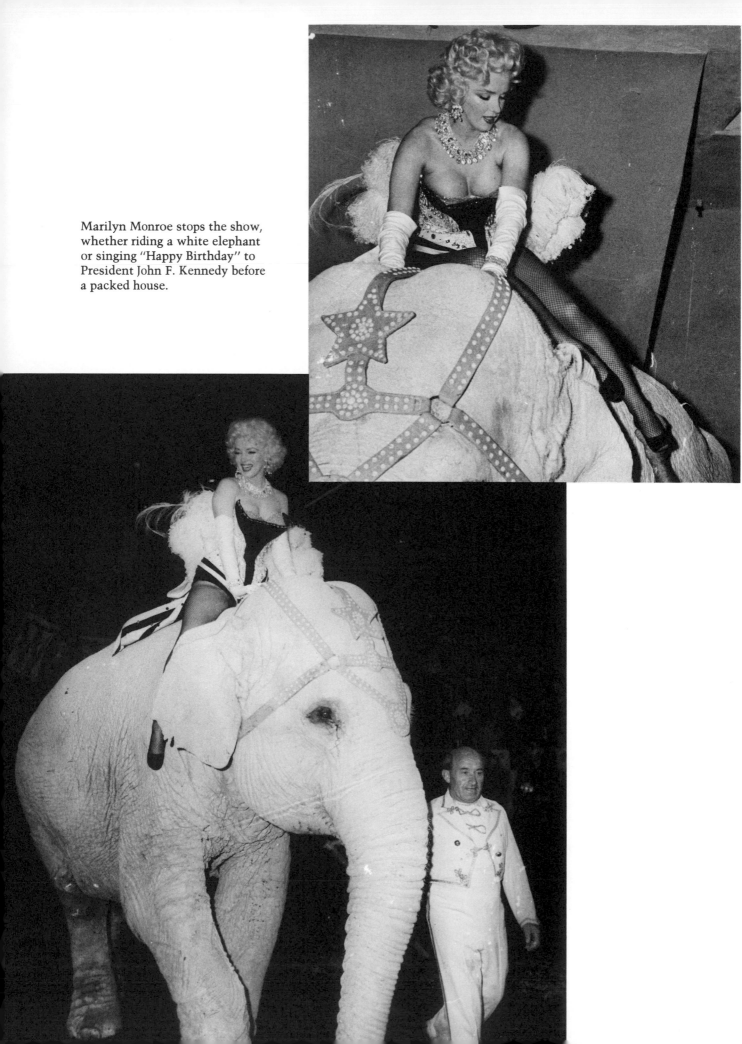

Marilyn Monroe stops the show, whether riding a white elephant or singing "Happy Birthday" to President John F. Kennedy before a packed house.

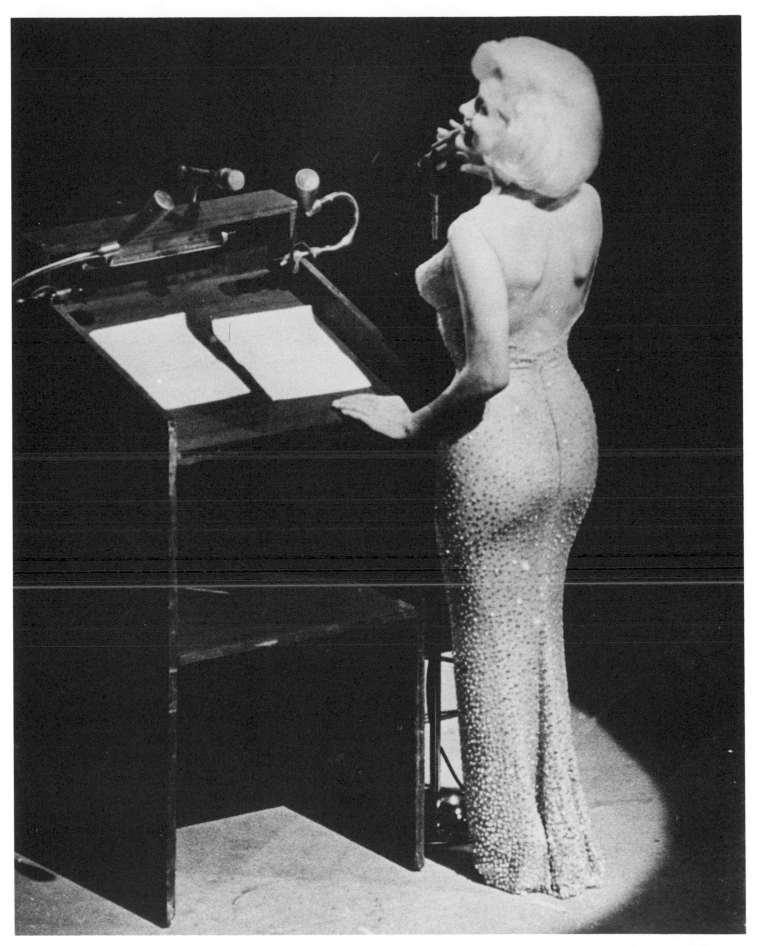

Another time a lion worked his way out of his cage during the night. No crisis then, either. A guard found him the next morning, sleeping in the stairwell.

But the liveliest "act" of the postwar years developed one evening during the dress rehearsal for the circus. One of the lions got confused and somehow trotted outside the chute leading into the big cage on the arena floor. John Goldner remembers: "I'm sitting there alongside the chute smoking my pipe when this lion walks past and heads for the lobby."

The big cat sniffed around the lobby awhile and was royally confused. By then, he was all too willing to be led someplace else. A brace of trainers drew him back into his cage before he could wander off into the audience. Later, the lion got his signals straight and found the right stage for the evening's opening performance.

One other memorable night was provided by a pair of baby elephants, the stars of the final act of the show. They were decked out in top hats and white dickeys, a couple of real gentlemen in the big town. But they gave the act an unexpectedly smashing finale. They broke loose, rumbled into the main lobby, and smashed into the wall with their shoulders, tearing out a large chunk of the inside of the building.

Then they bounced out into Fiftieth Street and moved along the roadway—against traffic. Back down Forty-ninth Street they came—also against traffic. Even in the jungle of New York traffic, you don't often encounter elephants going the wrong way on a one-way street.

They finally were corralled by a posse from the circus and were tied to a pole outside Murphy's Bar. And anybody who happened to be leaving the bar just then walked smack into an unforgettable sight—a pair of baby elephants in top hats.

The years after the war may not have been so "roaring" as the years after the earlier war, but they provided the public with the same sort of plunge into free-for-all leisure, whether it meant parachuting, skiing in the Rockies, soaring over Elmira, boating on Narragansett Bay, or spending money to hear Frank Sinatra, watch basketball, or bet on boxing.

People were so relentless in their rush to recreation that they were stopped by neither rain nor snow nor gloom of night. Especially not by snow. When twenty-six inches buried New York during the Christmas holidays of 1947, the city lay paralyzed for days. But on the very night when the blizzard struck, on December 26, the Garden opened the doors for a tennis match, of all things. It featured Jack Kramer in his debut as a professional and Bobby Riggs, who had just beaten Don Budge for the number-one ranking after both players had returned from their military service.

In spite of the fact that the match was scheduled at the wrong time in the wrong place and even in the wrong season, the Garden sold 16,052 tickets for the event the day after Christmas. Then it started snowing, and it kept snowing for twenty-four hours. But Kramer and Riggs played a bristling four sets before Riggs won by 6–4, 10–8, 4–6, and 6–4. And in the galleries? Well, on a night fit for neither man nor beast, when planes were grounded and trains were unreported, on the night of the avalanche, 15,114 souls trudged through drifts to the Garden to watch. Only 938 stayed away.

There were other nights when not many stayed away, even without the challenge of a blizzard. They came for dogs, cats, horses, clowns, preachers, even mayors. They saw Henry Armstrong win his third world championship and John Thomas jump seven feet for the first time. Bill Mosienko of the Chicago Black Hawks scored three goals in twenty-one seconds there. The Duke and Duchess of Windsor met Emmett Kelly there, and Marilyn Monroe rode a pink elephant there. And Fiorello La Guardia conducted the Sanitation Department Band there. A circus clown was even married there, and an elephant was drummed into service to present flowers to the bride.

But no "main event" there probably reached the shrieking success of the party that Mike Todd threw on October 17, 1957, to celebrate the first anniversary of his runaway film, *Around the World in Eighty Days.*

The idea, the producer announced, was to throw a party "for a few of my intimate friends." In pursuit of this modest goal, Todd rented the entire house and provided gifts that ranged from motorcycles to an airplane while television cameras recorded the intimacy of the event.

Entertainment was supplied by acrobats, animals, mummers' string bands, and folk dancers. Todd's wife, Elizabeth Taylor, served as the official hostess. But she fought a losing battle as thousands of persons poured down from the reserved seats

The six-day bicycle race returns from exile and stages the same old grind on a new curved track. . . .

. . . Glenn Cunningham, whose legs were severely burned when he was an 8-year-old child in Kansas, wins the Wanamaker Mile six times. And professional tennis supplies a new generation of stars: Pauline Betz Addie returning a backhand while Pancho Segura watches and Gussie Moran and Jack Kramer brace in the far court.

Through all the changes, and all the Gardens, two things remain: the horse show and the dog show. Horses and riders come to attention as the band signals another opening.

In a century of blue ribbons, not many dogs outperform the boxer Ch. Bang Away of Sirrah Crest, winner of more than 100 best-in-show awards, including the 1951 Westminster.

like Gothic tribes and destroyed a monstrous cake that had taken twenty days to bake. Gate-crashers helped themselves to the gift motorcycles and rode them straight out the doors. Ushers working as waiters began to sell dozens of bottles of champagne that Todd had intended to give away. Drunks climbed onto the wings of the gift airplane and seesawed them until they broke. And Duke Ellington tried, without success, to impose at least a ceremonial degree of order by striking up his band with "The Star-Spangled Banner."

Reporting the chaos in the *New York Times* later, Murray Schumach suggested that Todd's party "for a few intimate friends" had rapidly deteriorated into "a melee that resembled the decline of the Roman Empire." And Mike Todd, Jr., later remembered:

"It was a riot. The next morning, Dad was making himself

For absolute chaos, no event probably surpasses the party thrown in 1957 by Mike Todd, the film producer. Gate-crashers storm the arena, plundering it like vandals, and *The New York Times* reports that the melee resembles "the decline of the Roman Empire."

some eggs when his lawyer and accountant showed up. He said, 'Okay, give me the bottom line.' They told him it was about $400,000. He said, 'I should have been arrested.' "

If any expiation of these sins was possible, it may have taken place on the more dignified evenings when the annual Hanukkah Festival for Israel was held, with the least expensive seats in the steep balcony going for $100 apiece and choice seats going for $1,000 in Israeli bonds. Or it may have taken place when Billy Graham occupied the pulpit for an entire summer and delivered the message to a total of 1,687,000 believers.

But chances are that nothing could fully atone for the howling mob scene generated by Mike Todd's $400,000 bash. Nor could anything fully measure the parade of events that swirled through the place on other nights, though Grantland Rice tried to measure it once in these lines of half-verse.

> Fighters and elephants, lions and gorillas,
> Basketball players now seven feet tall,
> Left hooks and uppercuts, wild steers and cowboys,
> Famous Big Bill with his slash at the ball,
> Queen Henie, Louis, and bicycle riders,
> Hockey, a song, or a punch in the snoot.
> Runners and jumpers and trapeze performers. . . .
>
> So the wild scramble rolls dizzily on.
> Noise, sweat and color and action unending,
> What a weird mixture of all that can happen!
>
> Bring on the Benzedrine.
>   I need a drink. . . .

The American Legion stages some memorable gatherings, too. And in a house of rallies, Kansas rallies round its favorite son, Dwight D. Eisenhower.

10 FIGHT NIGHT

"The Garden meant boxing," Harry Markson was saying, not bothering to eulogize the elephants, acrobats, dancers, milers, skaters, or seven-foot centers who also worked there. "In Liverpool, Buenos Aires, or Tokyo, or anyplace in the world.

"I went to Rome in 1968 to sign Nino Benvenuti for a return match with Emile Griffith, and while I was there, the Benvenuti family had an audience with the pope. About 5,000 people were there in the Vatican, and a few of us very special guests up front. Imagine it: St. Peter's, all the art treasures and religious meaning, priests and monsignors and cardinals all over the place, and there I was, too. It was kind of unbelievable, like another world.

"Then I was introduced to Pope Paul as Harry Markson of Madison Square Garden. And the pope stepped back, his face lit up, and he sort of exclaimed, 'Ah, Madison Square Garden—boxing.' "

People, let alone popes, didn't always have such a clear-cut picture of the onetime "central palace of pleasure" in Manhattan. Sometimes not even presidents of the Garden had such a clear-cut picture. During the Depression once, when John Reed Kilpatrick was running the place, he groped for an imaginative idea to broaden the horizons and the cash flow of the arena, and came up with a doubleheader, a combination program. Half of it featured motorbike races, half featured the Hall Johnson Choir.

"They started the evening with the choir," Markson remembered. "But it became a very embarrassing thing right away. After all, you had two extremely different sets of customers

Golden age: Sugar Ray Robinson, five times the middleweight champion, takes the right hand from Carmen Basilio.

there that night. And the people who came to see the motorbike races weren't particularly interested in the Hall Johnson Choir. The next thing you knew, they were up yelling, 'Bring on the races, let's go.'

"You know, the General wanted to do something for the choir, so he scheduled it into the Garden. And he wanted to do something for the Garden because of the Depression, so he scheduled the doubleheader. But it turned into a fiasco, and he said he'd never reach out like that again."

He didn't, and a few years later, prompted by the era of Joe Louis and the revival of boxing, things grew clear-cut again. Even Harry S. Truman made it there one night in early 1945 for the Rocky Graziano–Billy Arnold fight. That was the main event, and it was preceded by a bruising prelim between Tony Janiro and Marty Pignatore. It was a rousing fight, chiefly because Janiro was beautiful to watch, a rare mixture of fighter and puncher at work. And when he had finished, he stepped through the ropes and came down the steps to walk through the aisle to his dressing room.

As he did, a man sitting at ringside jumped up from his chair and shook hands cordially and admiringly with him. Later, when Tony got to his locker room, he asked who the hand-shaker was. His manager, Frankie Jacobs, replied, "He's the Vice-President."

And Tony, who possessed an absolutely clear-cut vision of his world, was properly impressed.

"Holy gee," he said, conceding the point. "Imagine that. The vice-president of Madison Square Garden."

One month and three days later, Harry Truman became president, and not of Madison Square Garden.

In the twenty years before Tony Janiro shook hands with Harry Truman, from 1925 to 1945, from Dempsey's day to Louis, the Garden supplied the stage for thirty-two championship fights. Seven involved the heavyweight title and all of those involved Louis—against Nathan Mann, John Henry Lewis, Arturo Godoy, Johnny Paychek, Red Burman, Buddy Baer, and Abe Simon. Final score: 7 to 0, Joe.

Next came the light-heavyweights: Tommy Loughran against Mike McTigue, Bob Olin and Maxie Rosenbloom, Billy Conn against Melio Bettina, Gus Lesnevich and Anton Christoforidis, and Lesnevich against Tami Mauriello twice.

One middleweight title was decided between Tony Zale and Georgie Abrams; and three welterweight titles involving Barney Ross and Jimmy McLarnin, and Fritzie Zivic and Henry Armstrong. And the lightweights supplied some of the most memorable chain-reaction bouts of all: Tony Canzoneri defended the title against Al Singer, later regained it from Lou Ambers, and a year later lost it to Ambers, who then lost it to Armstrong. A year later, Ambers took it back from Armstrong, but a year after that he was knocked out by Lew Jenkins, who in turn lost it a year later to Sammy Angott.

Featherweight titles were won and lost, in some cases by men who later fought in upper divisions, by Canzoneri and Ross, Petey Sarron and Armstrong, Chalky Wright against Luke Constantino, and Willie Pep and Wright twice. In the bantamweight class, Lou Salica fought Sixto Escobar; and in the flyweight class, there were Midget Wolgast versus Black Bill and then Wolgast against Frankie Genaro.

There was so much action, at almost any weight, that the fight managers began to assemble in the lobby of the Forrest Hotel on Forty-sixth Street near Eighth Avenue, a couple of blocks from the Garden. And there, like vendors hawking their wares, they arranged the bouts that made other men's fame and fortune, swapping deals on a strip of unpretentious flooring that came to be known to the fight mob as Jacobs Beach.

"It lasted until the spring of 1949," Markson said, tracing the way of life along Jacobs Beach and the surrounding city streets.

> Mike suffered a stroke in '46, so Sol Strauss ran the show for two years—he was Mike's lawyer and also his cousin. Then, in 1948, I was made managing director of boxing at the Garden until the spring of 1949, when James D. Norris and Arthur Wirtz bought out Jacobs, formed the International Boxing Club, persuaded Joe Louis to retire, and started a tournament for his title.
>
> Norris was a big operator. His father owned a seat on the stock exchange, freighters on the Great Lakes, and property on Lake Shore Drive in Chicago. He bought the Olympia arena in Detroit for ten cents on the dollar, and also bought the Chicago Stadium and the St. Louis Arena. Young Jim Norris had Rocky Marciano coming along, too, and he controlled boxing for the next ten years. But it was a decade of skulduggery, and it finally ended when Judge Sylvester Ryan of the federal court in New York ruled that Norris's club was a monopoly that tied up championship fights.
>
> He ordered it dissolved, and Jim Norris resigned. Meanwhile, Norris and Wirtz had asked me to stay on when they took charge

of Garden boxing, and I was still there when they were forced to let go.

Another change took place behind the scenes in 1959, when Irving Mitchell Felt bought 40 percent of the Garden for what was reported to be less than $4 million. Later, the Graham-Paige Company, which Felt headed, bought 40 percent more. And so Felt became the prime force as the Garden headed through the postwar generation toward its fourth relocation in a century.

But alongside this prime force, the Garden encountered an irresistible force, television, which glorified and eventually cannibalized its basic force, boxing. Harry Markson reporting:

Boxing is always on a pendulum. Before TV, its success depended largely on the heavyweight champion. Joe Louis revived it during the Depression, and then Marciano carried it into the era of Floyd Patterson, Sonny Liston, and Ingemar Johansson. And by then, the pendulum had swung away and it needed somebody else to revive it again.

But meantime, television had revolutionized the whole industry after the war. Boxing lends itself to TV more than any other sport. All you have to do is focus a camera on a 20-foot square, and you've got a ringside seat.

It was introduced into the Garden by Mike Jacobs, though there had been a couple of demonstrations before the war. They were held in the RCA Building by John Royal, one of the broadcast pioneers of NBC. But as early as 1944, Jacobs signed a contract with the Gillette Company to do fifty fights a year, both radio and experimental TV. They carried the Chalky Wright–Willie Pep fight and announced that it was going on TV into hospitals for the servicemen.

Later, TV literally did bring boxing into millions of homes where it never had been seen before. If we had a controversial decision in a fight, thousands of letters would pour in, maybe 40 percent of them from women. You could tell it was a new audience. In the radio days, the letters started with "you thieving rats." But after TV came in, they'd open with "you incorrigible reprobates."

In the early days when radio carried the fights, Sam Taub was the ringside announcer and Adams hats served as the sponsor. Then Mike signed Gillette to the radio contract, and they handled the broadcasts for more than twenty years.

They even held a competition for the job of announcer, and some celebrated types like Paul Douglas, who later became a movie star, and others got into the auditions. It's amazing, though, how some small things decide big issues. One of the contestants was Don Dunphy, a radio announcer, who entered the auditions with the feeling that he didn't have a chance.

They held a kind of mass audition, and it was tough because they had to announce a fight between Gus Lesnevich and Anton Christoforidis—a couple of jaw-breaking names to pronounce, especially in fast action. Most of the announcers wrestled with the names, and it was a struggle. But Dunphy avoided the name problem by simply calling them Gus and Anton during the bout. Shrewd move, and when it was over, Dunphy won the job.

He also won a role in one of the longest-running shows in broadcasting, and thereby became a voice that reached American homes on a fixed schedule every Friday night for a generation. It was part of something called the Gillette Cavalcade of Sports, the first and biggest monolithic sports package on radio and TV, as regular as entertainment fixtures like Milton Berle or Ed Sullivan and the other early "habits" of the television era.

It traced its roots to the Maxon Agency of Detroit, which had been handling the Gillette advertising account since 1929. The plunge into sports was made in 1939, when the agency decided to sponsor the World Series, later adding the Kentucky Derby and Rose Bowl. Something was missing, though: a sport that cut across the seasons. So boxing joined the "cavalcade" in 1941, and a monster was born.

It came with a dual personality too. The radio broadcasts began in June of 1941 with Louis and Conn in the ring and Dunphy at the microphone; the television broadcasts began in September of 1944 with Pep and Wright up front and Jimmy Powers handling the microphone. Either way, the Garden staged the shows for a fee that, in those days at least, seemed astronomical, roughly $1 million a year for video alone. The sponsor supplied the money, the Garden supplied the tigers.

For a while, the only event that chased the fights off the screen was the annual arrival of the circus with its true tigers. But in 1955 that lapse in the schedule was adjusted by staging the fights outside New York during the circus days every spring. After that, if it was Friday night, it was "fight night."

The advertising way of life was so total that it even included special fights for special occasions. For example, the Gillette people knew that their best selling seasons for razor blades and other men's products fell around Father's Day and Christmas. No problem. They simply arranged with the Garden to promote

"Fight night" becomes an institution, and two of its charter members are James A. Farley, the Postmaster General and ringside regular, and Sugar Ray Robinson, whose dapper looks survive 202 bouts.

title fights in advance of those big commercial days, adding anywhere from $75,000 to $250,000 to the kitty. And so the public regularly could count on championship bouts early every June and December for the better part of twenty years.

The public also could count on certain regular members of the cast of characters every Friday night. The referee for many of the bouts was a metallurgist from St. Louis named Harry Kessler, who had already made a fortune by selling his steel-making process to giant corporations. Refereeing was a hobby, or an obsession, and Kessler atoned for it by donating his fees to charity. On other occasions, the "third man" might be Ruby Goldstein, who had won thirty-four of his own fifty-five fights by knockouts and sixteen others by decision. Later on, Arthur

Mercante directed traffic in the ring before parlaying his role into a second career as a television commentator.

The announcer in the ring was usually Johnny Addie, the successor to Joe Humphreys and Harry Balogh; and, like them, a master of the forced filibuster. He was so adept at ad-libbing the Queen's English that he could either stall for time or hurry to make up time at the nod of the television director. Once, Addie outdid himself. After announcing the national anthem, he found himself surrounded by silence because the tape recorder had broken down. So he rose to the occasion by standing there and singing the anthem himself, a feat that prompted one of the admiring fight-mob fanatics to observe, "Johnny just sang it *Acapulco.*"

Then there was "the man in the red baseball cap" at ringside, a Princeton graduate named Joel Nixon who became the producer of the television broadcasts in 1953 and who later became senior vice-president of the Garden for all its communications. He started wearing the baseball cap one night for the simple reason that the heavy headset that producers wore began to hurt his head. As Nixon recalls it:

> At the next fight, the referee came over and asked where my red baseball cap was. He liked it because it helped him spot the location of the cameras and announcers and, between rounds, he naturally wanted to stand in the neutral corner facing the cameras. So after that, I made certain that I wore it, and I became "the man in the red baseball cap."
>
> I wore it in a lot of places for a lot of years. We probably put on shows in thirty states in twenty years. Along the way, you could turn on the TV set and get fights in prime time almost any night of the week: Monday from St. Nick's Arena, Wednesday from out of town, Friday from the Garden on NBC-TV, later on Saturday over ABC-TV.
>
> One winter in the late fifties, there was a labor dispute at NBC involving the broadcast engineers. So we had to operate outside New York to avoid complications. We went to Syracuse, up in the snow belt, and spent eight weeks commuting from New York to Syracuse staging fights, with people trudging in the snow to the War Memorial Auditorium to watch fighters, mainly Latin Americans, who had never seen snow before. Everybody wanted to know why we hadn't settled on someplace like Miami Beach.
>
> There were other hazards, too. Once in 1953, Rocky Marciano fought Jersey Joe Walcott in their return match, and the sponsor put up an extra fee of $300,000 because it was for the heavyweight title. But it figured to be terrific for advertising. The only thing

was, the fight ended in just two minutes and twenty-five seconds. And this was before videotape, so we had no film to rerun; we just had to fill the air time for thirty minutes with chatter.

We took a bath, commercially speaking, even though Gillette got all kinds of sympathy from the press for spending so much money and getting so little exposure. Nobody wanted the fight to end in two and a half minutes, that's for sure. But Joe just wouldn't get up.

Another time, in 1955, Harold Johnson was fighting Julio Mederos. They were a contrast, because Johnson was a fine boxer who became the light-heavyweight champion and Mederos was a great big, slow-moving giant of a man. But at the start, Dunphy noticed that Johnson was behaving very strangely in the ring, and he had the guts to say so on the air, that Johnson was acting as though he'd been drugged or something.

Anyway, he was kind of out on a limb by saying it. But at the end of the first round, Harold sat down and then just slipped off his stool, and that was it. They said later that he had been sedated when somebody slipped him a section of loaded orange before the fight.

"So boxing thrived," Harry Markson said, taking up the story,

until the pendulum swung the other way and it started to decline. One reason was the fact that we became a sport infested with unsavory characters. But then, it often suffered from weak or phony regulation. Even back in the 1930s, the state boxing commission met twice a week—on *per diem.* They'd meet and collect the fee. On Tuesday, they'd suspend the wrestling champion, Dick Shikat. On Friday, they'd meet and reinstate him.

But another reason for the decline was overkill; boxing worked so well on TV that "fight night" became every night. After a while, you had TV shows in several cities on different nights of the week, with ordinary fighters like Tiger Jones and Gaspar Ortego in the ring and on the screen time and time again.

Finally, the TV ratings began to slip. And when the ratings slip, so does the network's interest.

The pendulum clearly needed another push, especially after the heavyweight title had been passed around among several fighters who did not capture the public's fancy: Floyd Patterson, Ingemar Johansson, Sonny Liston. And meanwhile, pro football was growing into a huge winner on the tube.

Just then, the pendulum was about to get its big push from a young fighter from Louisville who was winning the Olympic light-heavyweight title in the 1960 Games in Rome. It would take a few more years before he reached the professional scene and revived it beyond anyone's wildest imagination, but he was headed that way. He had size, speed, staccato combinations, fairy-tale charisma, and the unlikely name of Cassius Marcellus Clay.

Before Clay and his charisma arrived onstage, some corporate scene-changing was taking place backstage. It began taking place after Jim Norris had been ordered by the federal court to sell his stock in the Garden because of his monopoly control of boxing; he owned the fighters and the ring both.

But he no longer owned the swivel chair upstairs at the Garden. In the ripples that followed the court's ruling, the Graham-Paige investment company became the Madison Square Garden Corporation; its president, Irving Mitchell Felt, became chairman of the executive committee; Adm. John J. Bergen became chairman of the merger; and Ned Irish became president of its Madison Square Garden Division. Later, as the ripples continued, Bergen became honorary chairman and Felt took over as chairman and chief executive officer.

By now, Garden III could look back over nearly forty years of winners, losers, and record audiences.

For bicycle racing, the record was set during the opening days of the house, on Saturday, December 5, 1925, when Gerard Debaets and Alphonse Goosens won the final of the first six-day grind before 15,475. A little more than two years later, on Wednesday, February 29, 1928, track and field drew its biggest crowd, 18,252, for the Knights of Columbus Games, with Lloyd Hahn taking the featured mile run from Ray Conger and Dr. Otto Peltzer.

One year later, ice hockey set a record that would last as long as the arena; 18,120 persons paid to watch the Rangers lose to the Boston Bruins, 4 to 2, on Thursday, December 26, 1929. Some credit for preserving the record probably should go to the New York Fire Department, which later decided that the "safe" limit was 15,925.

It apparently didn't matter what day of the week was involved. Wrestling attracted its record crowd on a Monday, January 26, 1931. And not even the Depression could discourage the loyalists of Jim Londos. They saw him throw Jim McMillen and paid $59,469 for the joy of watching.

26TH. ANNUAL ALL STAR GAME

Sometimes "fight night" takes place when the main event is hockey, though not when the Garden is host to the All-Star Game and visiting demigods like Bobby Orr. . . .

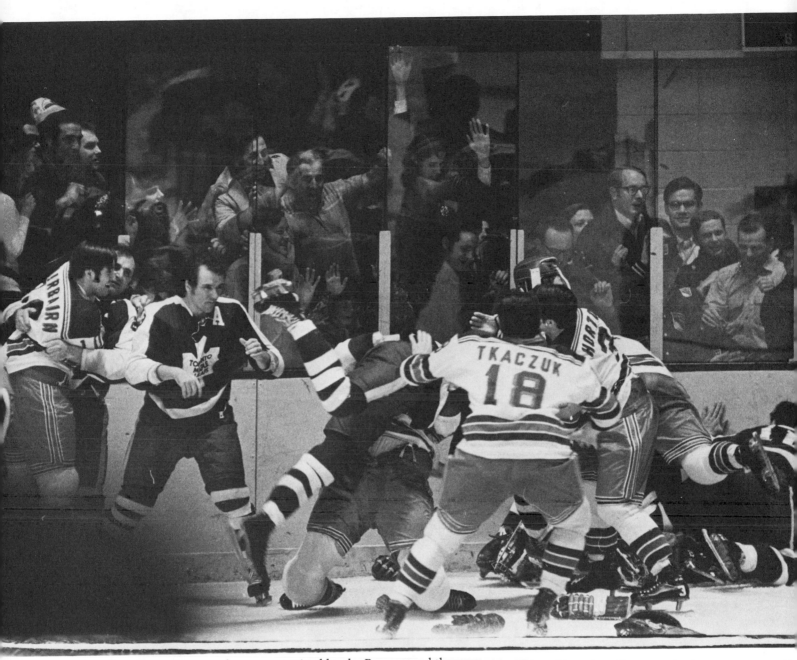

. . . At other times, sheer mayhem, as practiced by the Rangers and the
Toronto Maple Leafs.

The great one, Gordie Howe, plays
rough sometimes too . . . and
when the Rangers mix it up with
the Boston Bruins, these are the
times that try men's souls.

Goalies under fire: In triple overtime, the Rangers finally drive home the tie breaker against the Chicago Black Hawks and win it, 3 to 2. Meanwhile, the man in the mask for Notre Dame gives it the old college try with hand, foot and stick.

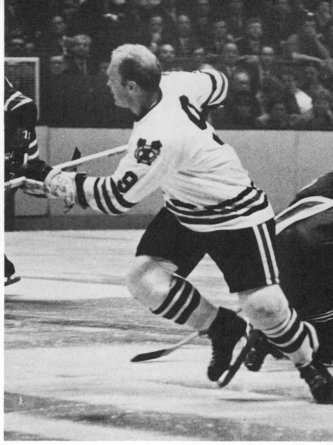

They are the good old days . . . days of triple-overtime drama . . . and of Bobby Hull . . . and, as Garden III closes in 1968 after 43 years, they are days of remembrance. Some old-time heroes return on skates for the final salute: Bun Cook, Bill Cook, Ching Johnson, Les Bourgault, Frank Boucher and Murray Murdoch.

Three years after that, on Saturday, April 14, 1934, the circus played to its biggest gate—17,108. And three years later, tennis had its biggest night; 17,630 went through the doors on Wednesday, January 6, 1937. The drawing card was Fred Perry of Britain, new to the scene, in a match against Ellsworth Vines.

After that, the house records were set as follows:

Ice Show: 15,663 attended Sonja Henie's Hollywood Ice Revue on Friday, January 28, 1938.

Rodeo: 12,998 paid to see the show on Saturday, October 12, 1940. The stars of the cast were Gene Autry, 200 cowboys, and 600 bulls, ponies, and broncos.

Boxing: 23,190 jammed the place on Friday, January 17, 1941. In the ring, Fritzie Zivic knocked out Henry Armstrong in the twelfth round and kept the welterweight title, which he had taken from Henry only three months before.

Basketball: 18,548 made it on Thursday night, March 14, 1946, for the quarter-final round of the NIT. They got their money's worth when Ernie Calverley heaved his famous 55-footer at the buzzer for Rhode Island State. The record for pro basketball, set regularly by the Knicks: 18,499. The total was strictly limited for crowd-control reasons. In fact, the same total was ordained for college ball, but they still managed to squeeze 49 more people into the hall the night Ernie let it fly.

Roller Derby: 16,877, on Thursday, June 8, 1950. The Jersey Jolters outskated, or maybe outshoved, the Brooklyn Red Devils by 24 to 22.

Why were so many of the records set in the early years of the Garden? Because after 1940 the management and the city officials got tougher and imposed tighter limits.

But after 1940 the stage set and the props became more sophisticated, especially in the years after the war. As a result, one capacity crowd could be followed by another in a day-night doubleheader. All it took was a little magic in the Garden, plus some fast footwork by the crew in the arena.

Protecting the spectators became a small science too, when hockey pucks began flying over the boards and into the lower seats. That particular problem was solved, or at least eased, when the Garden installed a glass screen along the contour of the rink. It was done in October, 1946, just in time for the opening of the season, and the box-seat clientele probably never realized the marvel that stood between them and the ice.

It was Herculite tempered plate glass, five-eighths of an inch thick, heated in a furnace at 1,700 degrees Fahrenheit, rising two feet above the boards (which were three and a half feet high). But if you happened to be sitting behind the goal, in the no-man's-land of hockey, you had a full five feet of plate glass for extra comfort. The paneling was constructed in five-foot sections and was installed even before the crowd had left the arena from the previous event.

How impenetrable was it? The science people figured that, to shatter the surface of the glass, a person with an ice pick would have to hack away at one spot in the paneling for somewhere between twelve and twenty hours.

Two shots that did not bounce off or over the glass shield were fired by two of the finest hockey players who ever performed in the Garden; neither, as luck would have it, on the payroll of the house team. One was Maurice Richard of the Montreal Canadiens, who rammed home the 600th goal of his career as "the Rocket" on November 26, 1958. The other was Gordie Howe of the Detroit Red Wings, who got number 500 on March 14, 1962.

By then, both the net and the glass panel beyond it were living on borrowed time, along with everything else in the one-time trolley barn that Rickard had converted into his showplace almost four decades earlier. The news was made public on November 3, 1960, when Irving Mitchell Felt announced that another giant step was being planned—the construction of Madison Square Garden IV. Where and when would be decided later.

Two days later Felt received a note on the stationery of the Pennsylvania Railroad. It was from the assistant to the vice-president for real estate, J. W. Ewalt, and it read:

> Have noticed with interest your corporation's announcement of a proposed new Madison Square Garden. In the event you have not considered it, may we suggest as a possible site the "air rights" at Penn Station here in New York City. It is a two-block area (455' × 800') which can be available from the street level up. I believe you will agree that from a transportation standpoint, there isn't a better location in Manhattan.

Felt agreed. Eight months later it was settled. The Garden, having moved from Vanderbilt's old railroad shed on Madison Square to Stanford White's Moorish castle to Tex Rickard's blockhouse on the West Side, now would reach in a new direction—straight up.

It would rise above Penn Station, the rail center of the Northeast, and its network of tracks belowground at Thirty-third Street between Seventh and Eighth avenues, seventeen blocks south. But the most radical change was not one of location or altitude or design; it was one of concept. The new Garden would embrace sports, popular entertainment, business offices, theaters, and expositions. The price was radical too—$116 million.

They started pulling apart Penn Station on October 28, 1963, and began pouring concrete on May 1, 1964. They were thinking of a circular building for the Garden, alongside a twenty-nine-story skyscraper. They were still four years from opening, but they were thinking big.

While the dreamers were dreaming, the people running the show were still trying to make ends meet downstairs. And for the boxing department, that meant the old "pendulum problem," the swing away from the heavy traffic of the fight-night years. And the best chance anybody had of shoving the pendulum back lay with the Olympic champion from Louisville, Cassius Clay.

During the same summer of 1960 when Clay was winning his Olympic title, Floyd Patterson was making history by becoming the first man to regain the heavyweight championship. He did it by knocking out Ingemar Johansson in the fifth round at the Polo Grounds. He repeated the performance, in six rounds, at Miami Beach nine months later. But a year and a half after that, Patterson was wiped out in the first round in Chicago by the giant Sonny Liston. And a year after that, Liston repeated the performance in Las Vegas: one round, and good-bye Floyd.

The chief trouble with all that knocking out was that none of the participants really caught the public's imagination. Patterson supposedly had soul, Liston obviously had size, but neither had the star quality that turned champions into heroes. Then on February 25, 1964, Clay overpowered the favored Liston in six rounds in Miami Beach—at least Sonny didn't answer the bell for the seventh—and the pendulum began to swing back.

There still weren't many good fighters around, but Clay quickly made up for the shortage by drawing attention to his own personality. He was an outstanding talker as well as an outstanding fighter. In 1965 he demolished Liston again in one

round with one punch, though not everybody remembered seeing the punch. He also took Patterson out in the twelfth round. Then in 1966 he cut his way through five opponents, the way Joe Louis used to do during his "bum-of-the-month" days: George Chuvalo by a decision in Toronto, Henry Cooper in six in London, Brian London in three in London, Karl Mildenberger in twelve in Frankfurt, Germany, and Cleveland Williams in three in Houston.

None of that was too spectacular by itself, but it was good enough for Harry Markson and his matchmaker, Teddy Brenner. They imported Clay to the Garden on March 22, 1967, his debut in the house after much traipsing around Europe, and he obliged by knocking out Zora Folley in seven.

A short time later, Clay—who adopted the name Muhammad Ali—refused to be drafted into the army and, as a result, was stripped of his title. But that proved to be only the beginning of his career as an international superstar, a rank he would establish four years later in Irving Mitchell Felt's new circular dream.

Meanwhile, they finally broke down the ring in the Garden on December 15, 1967, after Luis Rodriguez won a ten-round decision over Benny Briscoe. That was the final fight in Rickard's favorite haunt, but this time nobody thought to sing "Auld Lang Syne" when the lights went out.

Yet another Garden is rising, and with it comes another superstar: Muhammad Ali.

11 GARDEN IV
All the World's a Stage

As stages go, this one wasn't exactly skimpy, not even by Barnum's soaring standards of a century earlier; a lavish main arena with 20,234 seats arranged on colored terraces and surrounded on different levels by half a dozen auditoriums, theaters, and forums.

It was a circular building that rose thirteen stories above the street and extended 425 feet in diameter and 153 feet high. It was a "complex," all right; so complex that they had to ring up the curtain in waves, almost by degrees.

They began on October 30, 1967, by opening the Bowling Center and its forty-eight lanes. Then on November 25, with the Welsh and Scots Guards on the bagpipes, they opened the Felt Forum with its 5,227 seats. On March 21 of the following year, they added the Exposition Rotunda with its first tenant, the Autorama-Cyclerama. Next came the Art Gallery on April 17.

The final flourish was a doubleheader opening—the Center Cinema and the Hall of Fame, which enshrined eighty-eight performers from the Garden's past, with others to be added in later years, maybe even later Gardens. The charter members covered a century in the old palace of pleasure, from John L. Sullivan in the prize ring to Anne Rogers Clark in the dog-show ring. They even included Barnum and Vanderbilt from the gaslight days.

But the sweep of history did its fanciest sweeping on the night of Sunday, February 11, 1968, when Garden IV went into business officially and ceremonially. It looked like opening

February 11, 1968: fourth home for the Garden is a circular "hatbox" built over Pennsylvania Station.

Opposite:
The opening card is neither a fight nor a bicycle race nor a basketball game. It's what they call these days a "spectacular." Bob Hope and Bing Crosby head the cast on stage.

night at the opera, with eleven escalators carrying most of the crowd of 19,832 first-nighters to their seats, where they watched at $10 to $250 apiece, many of them in formal dress.

The opening card was neither a fight nor a bicycle race, but the surest sign of the times: an entertainment spectacular led by Bob Hope and Bing Crosby while Phyllis Diller clowned from center stage, the West Point Glee Club sang, and Jack Dempsey and Gene Tunney shadowboxed through a slapstick revival of their celebrated fights of forty years before. Bob Hope even pulled on some pillow-sized mitts and sparred with Rocky Marciano while Crosby refereed. It was no better, no worse, than some of the fight-night bouts of the declining years of Garden III.

Actually, the old Garden stayed in business even beyond the opening of the new house. On Friday night of the busy weekend, Jim Ryun showed 15,002 track fans on Fiftieth Street how to do the mile in 3:57.5. Then on Saturday night, in their 550th home game, the Knicks fired a few parting shots at the old net and defeated the Philadelphia 76ers, 115 to 97. And on Sunday afternoon, while the black-tie crowd was gathering seventeen blocks south, the Rangers and Detroit Red Wings skated to a 3-all tie before the final 15,925 customers, and Jean Ratelle whacked home the final goal on Rickard's rink.

A few hours later, the new Garden was staging its celebrity gala, but even then there was a lot of commotion back at the old place. The Westminster Kennel Show was making its last stand uptown where a couple of thousand prize dogs were the last performers in the building. The last winner in the building was a Lakeland terrier named Champion Stingray of Derryabah.

Without missing a beat, the scene shifted for good to the "air rights" over Penn Station. On Wednesday, February 14, the Knicks beat San Diego in the first sports event in the new arena, and Walt Frazier scored New York's first points on a driving lay-up. However, that happened in the second game of a doubleheader; the first point "ever" had already been scored on a foul shot by Dave DeBusschere of Detroit, who later became one of the Knicks' stars of the 1970s.

One night later the program switched to college basketball, with Manhattan losing to Georgetown before NYU lost to Tulane. Then it was Friday, and the 100th New York AC track meet took over the place, with a new plastic-rubber surface re-

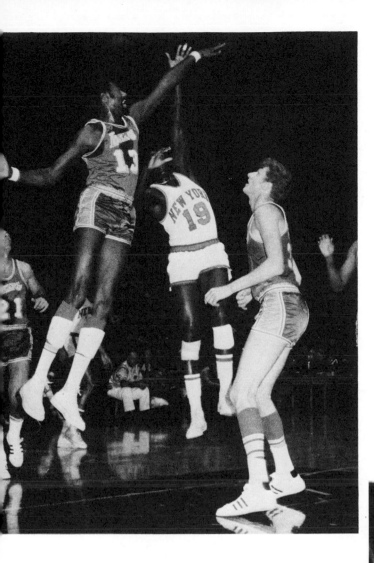

Captain, center and later coach of the team,
Reed leads a busy life on the boards,
surrounded by tall men. He takes the hook
shot against the leaping Wilt Chamberlain
and the watching Mel Counts. Whatever he
does, he keeps his eye on the large round ball.

Opposite:
There's a new emphasis on entertainment in
many forms in the new complex, but it still
includes the round ball. In 1970, it also
includes a championship basketball team. In
a dramatic play-off against the Los Angeles
Lakers, Willis Reed and Dave DeBusschere
overpower Elgin Baylor and lead the Knicks to
the title.

226

placing the old boards. And the inaugural week came to a close with pro basketball on Saturday night, the Knicks defeating Seattle, and with hockey on Sunday night, the Rangers beating Philadelphia. Bob Nevin scored the first goal for New York after Wayne Hicks had scored one for Philadelphia.

Then it was Monday, February 19, and no rest for the weary. The main fare was wrestling, and the main attraction was Bruno Sammartino, who marked the event by throwing Bull Ramos. The next night, with 19,500 in the seats, pro basketball returned to the scene, and the crowd itself set a record for the NBA. And so it went; you pay your money, you take your choice.

The first quick change was executed on Saturday, March 2, when 17,235 people watched hockey in the afternoon and 14,456 watched basketball at night. The Knicks dribbled on boards placed on top of the ice rink, which was being saved for a full program of hockey on Sunday afternoon and evening.

Boxing made its debut at a $100 top on March 4 with a title doubleheader. Nino Benvenuti beat Emile Griffith in the opener, and Joe Frazier stopped Buster Mathis in the finale. But the first winner in the new ring was a middleweight from Philadelphia named Dennis Heffernan, who scored a technical knockout over Tony Smith of the Bronx at 8:47 P.M., according to the people who held the stopwatches on such footnotes to history.

The first tennis tournament made the scene three weeks later, reaching its final round on Saturday, March 30, with 14,041 fans in the seats and Nancy Richey and Lt. Arthur Ashe in the winner's circle—as amateurs. But before they won their titles, the tennis court was lifted for a few hours to let the Knicks run across the wooden panels in a basketball game that was sandwiched into the schedule.

Three days later the circus arrived. But even elephants were giving ground in those days. They yielded the arena to hockey for three nights while the Stanley Cup joined the agenda. And if you couldn't get into the main arena to watch the Rangers, you could go next door and watch on closed-circuit television in the Felt Forum.

By then somebody had figured out that twelve heavyweight title fights alone had been staged in the old Garden and that 178 college basketball teams had played there. But the old order was passing for good and, on June 15, 1968, the new Garden took an

Opposite:
When Red Holzman talks, everybody listens, including Walt Frazier, Dave Stallworth and No. 24, a future United States Senator named Bill Bradley.

Opposite:
They call it "the fight of the century," but it's also the start of the era of high finance in fighting: the undefeated heavyweights Joe Frazier and Muhammad Ali. They are guaranteed $2,500,000 apiece, which may explain why the tumultuous signing ceremony is refereed by Harry Markson, the boss of boxing for the Garden.

early stride toward mass entertainment: pop music, with Herb Alpert and the Tijuana Brass raising the roof before a remarkable audience of 20,068. Cheering and paying.

One day in 1970, two men left the boxing office in Madison Square Garden, headed downstairs to Penn Station, and boarded a train for Philadelphia. They were Harry Markson and Teddy Brenner, and they had a mission: to sign the undefeated heavyweight champion, Joe Frazier, for a title fight against the undefeated ex-champion, Muhammad Ali.

The only fight that Ali had lost was to the selective service system, which had found him guilty of refusing to be drafted. The decision had cost Ali his title, but here he was, back again in business and building to the "fight of the century." All that Markson and Brenner needed to land the fight for the Garden was Joe Frazier's signature. Here's how Markson recalls it.

> When we got off the train in Philly that day, we were met by Joe and Yancey Durham, with a Cadillac. I was so impressed; it had an intercom.
>
> We drove to Joe Frazier's gym and went inside. The situation was that Frazier and Herbert Muhammad already had a deal for equal purses, with Herbert handling the business side for Ali. And the Astrodome in Houston also was bidding for the fight.
>
> It was an exercise in gamesmanship. We figured that the Astrodome people would figure that the Garden would bid $1,000,000 apiece. So they'd bid a little more: $1,100,000.
>
> So we went in and bid $1,250,000 apiece. And this was a lot of money, really unheard-of in those days. Anyway, as soon as we got to Philly, I telephoned Irving Mitchell Felt back at the Garden and said, "Mr. Felt, this fight's costing $2,500,000 in guarantees." He said, "Harry, do what you think is right."

Inside the gymnasium office, the financial sparring began immediately. Joe Frazier and Durham, his main man, seated themselves behind the desk, took out long yellow pads, and heard Markson say, "We'll guarantee each fighter a million and a quarter dollars."

At the words, furious activity broke out behind the desk. Both Joe and Yancey bent over their yellow pads and started writing. And they kept writing. Five minutes later they were still writing.

> They kept working away for a long time. And after a while, I stood up and began looking at the pictures on the wall. There was

229

March 8, 1971: "probably the
most glittering night ever held in
the Garden." In the fifteenth'
round of a furious fight, Frazier
suddenly and briefly floors Ali and
retains his championship on
points.

another long wait, and then Yancey yanked at Frazier's paper and
said, "Let me figure this out, Joe." And they got into another
round of furious figuring.

Finally, I got so curious that I kind of tiptoed around behind
them to take a peek. It was amazing and touching. They just didn't
know how to write down a figure as high as that $1,250,000. They
kept getting the commas in the wrong places, and they kept trying
it again.

After an even longer time, somewhere around six o'clock in
the evening, Joe's lawyer, Bruce Wright, telephoned with news
of a complication. A man named Jerry Perenchio had come in
with an offer: "He put down $200,000 cash to bind the fighters
for $2,500,000 each—double your offer."

But Wright added a further note: "At the insistence of Joe
Frazier and Yancey Durham, I've done one thing—tried to con-
vince him to put the fight in Madison Square Garden."

Perenchio was a forty-year-old Californian who once had
worked in his family's vineyard, which his father lost in 1944
during a price war. The family then moved to Los Angeles,
where Perenchio entered the business school at UCLA and did
some boxing in the intramural ring. "But I quit," he confessed
later, "when the same kids kept beating me up."

He played some golf too, but his closest brush with fame on
the course came when he worked once as a caddy for Howard
Hughes. But Perenchio persisted. He became a theatrical agent
and later president of Chartwell Artists, an agency that beat the
drums for Elizabeth Taylor and Richard Burton, Andy Williams,
Jane Fonda, Glen Campbell, and Henry Mancini and that promoted the practice of concert appearances on college campuses.

Perenchio also engineered a few sizable deals in his time,
including the sale of Caesar's Palace in Las Vegas for $83 mil-
lion. But even in Las Vegas, where Barbra Streisand reportedly
commanded a million dollars, it took some doing to underwrite
a single engagement featuring Muhammad Ali and Joe Frazier in
"the fight of the century."

However, Las Vegas had been the site of Ali's assault on
Floyd Patterson in 1963, a match that drew all of 7,816 customers but that in turn generated $4,747,690 in total receipts. And
two years later, they had met in a rematch that drew 412 *fewer*
persons but that still did $3,570,000 worth of business. The rea-
son was that many more people had paid to watch the fights

over closed-circuit television far from the Strip, and the lesson was not lost on Jerry Perenchio.

He still needed a bankroll, though, and he found one in Jack Kent Cooke, who once had traveled door-to-door selling encyclopedias for $39.50 a set. And when that didn't work, which was often, Cooke had earned his keep by playing the saxophone in a dance band. But by 1970, he was earning his keep in bunches: partner to Lord Thomson in newspapers, radio stations, and cable television; part owner of the Washington Redskins football team; full owner of the Los Angeles Lakers basketball team, the Los Angeles Kings hockey team, and the Inglewood Forum. He also owned a $28,000 Bentley, half a dozen other luxury cars, and a mansion in Bel Air.

The alliance was made. "This fight," reasoned Perenchio, "is entertainment. It's like *Gone with the Wind.* You could show it on the side of a supermarket, and people would come to see it."

It took him ten minutes to decide to take the plunge, and it took him a few hours to persuade Jack Kent Cooke, whom he had never met, to take it with him. Cooke put up $4,500,000, got a letter of substantiation from the Chase Manhattan Bank, and got the other $500,000 from Madison Square Garden. The deed was done.

The anatomy of the monster deal looked like this: The Garden would sell out, 19,000 strong, with tickets scaled from $20 in the rafters to $150 at ringside, for a live gate of $1,250,000. But that would provide only one-quarter of the two fighters' purses. Half a century before, the live gate would have been the only gate; now, though, it was merely the tail that wagged the dog.

"The live gate is not the primary factor," Perenchio observed. "The closed-circuit TV network *is.* We expect to have a million and a half seats in the United States and Canada at a minimum of $10 a seat. That's a potential of $15,000,000, plus the foreign sales around the world."

"I'm a traditionalist," he added, as though rationalizing their choice of the Garden for the big show. "I'm a cornball. I believe if you have the biggest fight in history, you should have it in the greatest boxing arena in the world."

They had the biggest fight, all right. They grossed $18,000,000, of which $1,200,000 was collected at the gate from the splashy throng of 20,455, a sideshow in itself: men wrapped in mink coats, women loaded with jewels and spangles, astronauts like Alan Shepard, actors like Marcello Mastroianni, politicians of all ranks and all hues, general celebrities like Frank Sinatra and David Frost, athletes and tycoons of business, and platoons of people named Kennedy.

"The buildup had started long before that night," Harry Markson said, retracing his steps from Joe Frazier's gym in Philadelphia.

> When we made the announcement at Toots Shor's, there was a mob scene, a crush that we couldn't control. Then when Ali arrived at the Garden for the weigh-in, the day of the fight, he couldn't even get through the thousands of nuts outside. There was chaos everywhere.
>
> We finally decided it would be better if he didn't try to leave the building at all—just stay there until the fight. So I went to his people, mainly Herbert Muhammad, and asked if he'd mind if Ali stayed inside. They said okay, so we furnished a small barracks for him inside the Garden. We brought in cots, television sets, food, enough of everything for a dozen people to live out the day while Ali was napping all afternoon. It worked out fine, except that I later got a bill from the Penn Plaza people who catered the sleep-in—a bill for 100 people.
>
> Then just before the fight that night, Drew Bundini showed up with 200 people at the employees' entrance to the Garden. He said: "We got Ali's trunks and equipment and all his stuff here. We don't get in, he don't fight."
>
> So the guys at the gate telephoned upstairs for help, and I came running down and we had this big powwow. But still Bundini wouldn't budge. He was part of Ali's inner circle, and this time he had plenty of company. The only thing we could do was make a deal. We'd let twenty of them in, even though they didn't have tickets and we didn't have a foot of room inside.
>
> But they were Ali's army from uptown, they were the camp crowd, they were the poor people. We agreed that twenty could come in, the gate was opened, and about fifty of them rushed through and disappeared in the crowd.

Inside the arena, the tension was electric as the evening built toward its peak, which arrived when Ali and his ring entourage nudged their way through the crowd. He didn't disappoint them either, not in the way he was dressed or in the way he cavorted. He was wrapped in a white robe with a hood, and he was bursting with energy, taunting Joe Frazier, flicking his fists at Joe as they passed each other in the ring, firing both hands at Joe after the bell sent them out for "the fight of the century."

It was a classic, fifteen rounds of nonstop action, with Frazier hurling overhand bombs and Ali finding the range with stinging jabs and left-right combinations. Ali took the lead in the early rounds as Frazier kept boring straight ahead, taking dozens of pinpoint punches and then retaliating with his own heavy hooks. He was six and a half inches shorter than Ali in reach but as solid as a blockhouse.

A classic, and one that ended with a memorable final round and a sweeping left hook by Frazier that knocked Ali onto his seat. He bounced up, and they finished as they had started, head to head, firing at all ranges, hitting all targets. When it was over, the winner of the close, tigerish, and historic fight was Joe Frazier.

"It was," Markson observed, "probably the most glittering night ever held in the Garden."

For a while the man who scheduled the acts was Alvin Cooperman, who came from the theater and television and who reached into the far corners of his show-business imagination to keep other evenings glittering. The old standby, the Ringling Brothers and Barnum & Bailey Circus, soon was joined by rock-'n'-roll troupes, a Disney carnival that ran most of one summer, the Mrs. Black America pageant, the Moscow Ice Show with Russian bears playing hockey on skates, and the old roller derby. One night 400 professional motorcycle racers took over the boards and whipped around the arena for $25,000 in prize money while the customers paid from $4 to $7 to watch them climb the walls.

Sometimes the action was supplied by tall men with basketballs, men like the 1969–70 Knicks. The coach then was Red Holzman, who had succeeded Dick McGuire, and the men on the court were Willis Reed at center, Walt Frazier and Dick Barnett with their sleight-of-hand at guard, and Dave De-Busschere, Cazzie Russell, and Bill Bradley up front. They were intelligent types and they played together, and during one stretch they won eighteen straight games.

They won sixty of their eighty-two games that season, eliminated Baltimore from the play-off in seven games, knocked off Milwaukee in five, then faced Wilt Chamberlain, Jerry West, and the Los Angeles Lakers for the championship. Each team won a game in the Garden; each team won a game in Los Angeles, both in overtime.

They come from all walks of life, whether they are Irving Mitchell Felt, president of the Garden, or Commander Whitehead, globetrotting celebrity, or Emile Francis, ringleader of the Rangers.

It's a century after Barnum herded his first elephants through Madison Square, but animals are still headliners in the Garden: feeding elephants, trained bears, horses prancing in the ring.

Back in New York, they went at it again, but on one play the Knicks suddenly lost their big man. Reed, driving for the basket, strained a muscle in his side and was gone. It was unthinkable, but somehow they rallied from ten points down, pulled the game out, and flew back to California one game away from the title. But without Willis, they were without armor. And while Chamberlain poured in forty-five points with twenty-seven rebounds, the Lakers overpowered them and tied the series.

Then they were back in the Garden for the final shoot-out on May 8, the Knicks flanked by 19,500 screaming fans but minus their captain and hero, Willis Reed. That is, they were minus him until he made a dramatic appearance on the court while the teams were warming up, limping out in his game uniform, barely able to walk or shoot, and apparently not at all able to play.

But when they lined up, Willis was there. And although he moved slowly and with pain, he somehow popped in the first two baskets as the roaring became thunderous. They ran and shot and scored, they led all the way, and with a crippled center playing against one of the deepest and most talented teams in basketball history, they won their title in storybook style.

Now they were all into the decade of the seventies, and the storybook style was becoming a way of life, especially after the arrival in the summer of 1973 of a new ringmaster, Michael Burke.

He was tall and smartly turned out, and he had some tall credentials: running back in football at the University of Pennsylvania, officer in the navy in World War II, secret agent behind enemy lines in Europe, general manager of the Ringling Brothers and Barnum & Bailey Circus, scriptwriter in Hollywood, vice-president of the Columbia Broadcasting System, and president of the New York Yankees.

When he left the Yankees that summer, after seven years of rebuilding the best team in baseball, Burke considered a life of contemplation far from the crowded canyons; maybe Ireland, where he could spend his time writing his memoirs, which would read like fiction.

But his scheme was disrupted by a telephone call that invited him to a meeting with Charles Bluhdorn, chief man at the Gulf + Western Corporation, the controlling stockholder in Madison Square Garden. Bluhdorn suggested a very different sort of effort

Michael Burke takes over in 1973 with a purpose: "to produce entertainment in the broadest sense."

for Burke: president of the Garden. For a while Burke wasn't sure. He really didn't care much for the purely business aspects of the job, such as the real estate and hotels that were owned by the company. But he was intrigued by sports and entertainment, and he had often observed that he'd rather be a lamppost in New York than the mayor of Chicago—or anyplace else.

That was okay with Gulf + Western, which signed him to a five-year contract as senior vice-president of the Garden for sports and entertainment. Actually, he became the president of the Garden Center, meaning the show-business side of the business, while a tax lawyer named Alan Cohen succeeded Irving Mitchell Felt as president of the corporation.

"The Garden was too sprawling and fragmented in its organization," Burke recalled. "It needed an overhaul. Society was changing its tastes, and we had to produce entertainment in the broadest sense. Not just locker-room sports, but it had to become a center of family entertainment.

"We're dealing now with a lot of different publics. We pay $15,000 a day in real-estate taxes, before opening the doors. So we have to deal with the broadest possible audience. We have to draw more than 5,000,000 people inside just to pay the bills."

The basketball audience was still there, and so was the hockey audience, but that took care of only about 80 nights of the year. Burke promptly took some new tacks, starting with a contemporary-music unit that booked rock concerts with performers like Bob Dylan, the Grateful Dead, the Bee Gees, Yes, and other headliners.

"There are millions of kids out there who dig it," he reflected, "so we've got to give it to them."

Then came the ethnic festivals—Polish, Puerto Rican, black, whatever. And when a tiny Russian named Olga Korbut made gymnastics a mass sport, or entertainment, or happening, they created something called the America Cup, fourteen nations competing in the biggest concentration of gymnasts outside the Olympics. The Romanian sprite Nadia Comaneci competed *before* she became the star of the 1976 Olympics.

Then the Garden got into cable television, a move that relayed the new and old features across forty states under the title "Madison Square Garden Presents." It presented more than 150 events a year to people around the country far from the scene.

Sometimes the star performer is a
child, like Nadia Comaneci, the
Rumanian sprite and gymnastics
prodigy, who dazzles the world at the
1976 Olympics.

The idea was very simple. If you can't bring all those people to the show, bring the show to all those people.

"The two most differing crowds we have," Burke said, "are the horse-show crowd, which comes in top hats and formal dress, and the wrestling crowd, which comes as it is. If you stopped 100 people on Fifth Avenue and asked if they still had wrestling at the Garden, they'd say no—not in a long time. But they'd be wrong. There's a wrestling public too, and one Monday night every month we revive it—and draw 20,000 people, with an overflow into the Felt Forum."

There was also a tennis public, and Burke set out to corral it, too. When Suzanne Lenglen and Vinnie Richards had introduced professional tennis to the Garden fifty years earlier, the sport was still considered a class event rather than a mass event. But now the pros were crisscrossing the world in pursuit of millions in prize money, and a whole new generation of amateurs was playing tennis on public courts, domed courts, and club courts.

To join this stampede, Burke booked the Grand Prix Masters tournament into the Garden in January 1978, but it wasn't easy. "It took us two years to land the tournament," he remembered, "and even then we needed help. But we got it from a 'friend in court,' you might say: Jack Kramer, who had played in that match against Bobby Riggs thirty years before, the night of the great blizzard. Jack helped us line up the players and stage the tournament, and it finally opened to the largest crowd in tennis history."

The winner was Jimmy Connors, who was forced to quit the second Grand Prix Masters a year later in January 1979 because of a foot injury. But, with $400,000 in prize money at stake, the tournament moved to a dramatic finish with nineteen-year-old John McEnroe barely beating thirty-five-year-old Arthur Ashe.

For sheer mass and glitter, though, no event rivaled the Ali-Frazier fight as much as the Democratic National Convention of 1976. It didn't grind on for two weeks like the Democratic marathon of 1924. In fact, when the delegates gathered on Mon-

Sometimes the star is a young millionaire pro, like Jimmy Connors, who wins the first Grand Prix Masters tennis tournament in the Garden in 1978.

Sometimes the performers are watched by the V.I.P.'s of public life as fans: John V. Lindsay, while Mayor of New York, takes time out to watch. Henry Kissinger, the Secretary of State, signs autographs like any other star. And Abraham D. Beame, another Mayor with an eye on the arena, follows the Rangers and supplies the popcorn.

And sometimes the V.I.P.'s of public life become the performers on stage. Fifty-two years after the Democrats needed 103 ballots to nominate John W. Davis, they return to the Garden in force, with heavyweights like Hubert H. Humphrey. And this time they need only one ballot to nominate Jimmy Carter.

day, July 12, Jimmy Carter of Georgia already had enough votes —pledged votes or primary-election votes—to guarantee the nomination.

But this was the age of happenings, and the party's planners and the television networks spared no imagination in staging this particular happening. The Democrats got the ball rolling by spending $250,000 to hire a company to rearrange the Garden for the immense logistics involved. Then an army of carpenters, electricians, and technicians swarmed over the building to provide space and communications for 3,000 delegates, in red seats facing the podium, and for the 10,000 newsmen from 700 daily papers and radio and television stations around the world.

"A lot of people were skeptical about our using a sports arena," said Robert S. Strauss, chairman of the party. "But now when they see it, they realize that everybody in the hall will be a part of the convention. Madison Square Garden has proved to be the best kind of hall in which to hold a political convention."

To make certain that the tumultuous interruptions of the 1968 convention in Chicago were not repeated, the New York police thronged the area with 1,500 cops. In addition, Secret Service men attended in force, and 250 volunteer "convention aides" kept order in the aisles in blue blazers embroidered with patches that read: DNC 1976.

The only incongruous tone was supplied by a row of shrubbery and a slatted wooden fence along the front of the jammed podium in the center of things. They were installed, the stage director reported, to provide "a little bit of the flavor that was there in 1924."

But otherwise, the memories of the 1924 convention were overwhelmed. And on Wednesday night, July 14, Jimmy Carter overwhelmed the field by sweeping to the nomination on the first ballot and becoming the first presidential candidate of a major party from the Deep South since Zachary Taylor in 1848.

In 1978 Gulf + Western imported another ringmaster to broaden the horizons of the place even more. They owned 100 percent of the stock now and also controlled Roosevelt Raceway on Long Island and the Arlington Park racetrack in Chicago. And 650 events a year were being staged in the main arena of the Garden, in its rotunda, and in the Felt Forum. But even with all that razzle-dazzle, nobody was prepared for the arrival of the new impresario, David A. "Sonny" Werblin.

Like Burke, he came with tall credentials in show business. He had been president of the Music Corporation of America in the days when it served as the agent for movie stars, Hollywood queens, and the big bands. He owned racehorses, and he had created a revolution in professional football by signing Joe Namath out of the University of Alabama and then putting the New York Jets and the American Football League on the map. In a major-league sports sense, he had also put New Jersey on the map.

Werblin did that by taking command of the new sports complex in the Meadowlands across the Hudson River within sight of the Empire State Building and within sight of the established teams and racetracks in New York. He drew the Giants football team into the Meadowlands, and he almost drew the Jets there, until City Hall twisted enough arms to keep some semblance of order. He moved the Cosmos soccer team from Yankee Stadium into the huge new Giants Stadium, where they promptly created a sensation with international stars like Pelé, Franz Beckenbauer, and Giorgio Chinaglia and won two championships before sellout crowds.

He even built a racetrack where Thoroughbreds—in many cases expatriates from Belmont Park—ran at night, and a harness track where standardbred horses competed for $300,000 purses. When people asked if he felt guilty about raiding New York of its teams and animals, he replied:

"This isn't a War Between the States. This is one megalopolis with 26 million people. We're not stealing fans, we're creating them. If you paved the Hudson River, it would become Fourteenth Avenue."

He didn't pave the Hudson River, he crossed it. And when Sonny Werblin suddenly left his thriving sports complex in New Jersey to become president of the Madison Square Garden Corporation, it was the least likely thunderclap of a decade of thundering sports. General Lee had left the Confederacy to become the commander of the Union Army.

"Sonny Werblin's coming was really the final step in the overhaul of the Garden," Burke observed. "He combined all forms of entertainment in his experience."

He also combined the Garden's resources with his own imagination. He hired Fred Shero from the Philadelphia Flyers to run the Rangers, who now included the Swedish stars Ulf Nilsson

In 1978, a century after Barnum, a new impresario arrives: Sonny Werblin, a man for all seasons—show business, horse racing, football and, most recently, the all-sports complex across the Hudson River in New Jersey.

The big bands are there, with Duke Ellington at the keyboard . . .

. . . and the rock stars are there, with Mick Jagger raising the decibel
levels. . . .

. . . Paul McCartney is there
. . . and Bob Hope again
. . . and the one and only Elvis.

250

Camera hounds are there too, like Frank Sinatra and Bill Bradley, shooting the stars at work. . . .

. . . Then Frank goes to work while somebody else aims the camera.

and Anders Hedberg. To coach the Knicks he brought back Red Holzman, who had led them to their only two championships. He tried to sign Bill Walton as the team's center, then rebounded and signed Marvin Webster. He even imported his executive director from the Meadowlands complex, Jack Krumpe, once the president of the New York Racing Association.

Backstage, Dick Donopria was still setting the scene with nineteen engineers, thirteen electricians, three painters, seven carpenters, thirty stagehands, sixty utility men, and seventy cleaners. They were still building trestles for rock groups like the Rolling Stones, who obliged by bringing in their own stage with hydraulic wings that cost a quarter of a million dollars. And they were still installing acts like the Electric Light Orchestra, which dazzled the public with laser beams and a giant plastic spaceship shaped somewhat like a mushroom—an unidentified flying object that carried the whole orchestra above the arena.

They were climbing over the floor at eight o'clock in the morning to set up a rock show that wouldn't start until seven o'clock that evening. Then, after the show, they'd break it all down again for the next day's performance. If a track meet was next on the agenda, they would appear at three in the morning and work until the following noon, setting up the sprint track, the running track, the pole-vaulting pit, the high-jumping pit, and the shot-put course.

They were running ten or twelve events a week now, and sometimes they were busy picking up $3,000 worth of glass that the public had shattered in its frenzy trying to storm the doors to get inside.

Now the schedule listed things like the Knicks and Houston Rockets, the Rangers and Colorado Rockies, the People's Republic of China against Rutgers in basketball, the United States against Cuba in boxing, Neil Young and Crazy Horse in concert, the Oriental World of Self-Defense, the World Full Contact Middleweight Karate Title Bout between Butch Bell and Louis Neglia, the Commodores and O'Jays and the New York Salsa Festival, Jethro Tull with Uriah Heep, something called the Rock & Roll Spectacular Vol. XXV, a basketball team called the New Orleans Jazz and music groups that sounded like basketball teams, the Festival of Spanish TV Stars, the Stamp Festival, and the Silver Anniversary Japan Camera Show.

From John L. Sullivan to Johnny
Cash, the show goes on.

Also, the Harvest Championship Ball and, last but certainly not least, Jesus Loves New York.

It was all there under the same roof, opening the second century for the old "central palace of pleasure," a century that, Mike Burke predicted, would mark "a retreat from technology and a swing to people, not gadgets but performers, a place where people meet."

It was a hundred years and several leaps uptown and crosstown from the old days of dancing elephants, Vienna waltzes, exhibitions by the great John L. Sullivan, and Barnum's Monster Classical and Geological Hippodrome. And it was still, as *Harper's Weekly* had observed a century before, "a theatre, ballroom, restaurant, concert hall and summer garden . . . a sort of pleasure exchange."

And most of all, as the *New York Herald Tribune* had suggested, it was assuredly "not a building, but a state of mind."

Even Stanford White, who had helped to create both the building and the state of mind, would have agreed with that.

Not a building, but a state of mind.